More Praise for THROW OUT FIFTY THINGS

"It is as unsurprising as it is exciting that Gail delivers a pragmatic guide for not just uncovering, but discovering your best 'self.' Gail's wisdom inspires us to shed the physical and mental clutter that too often weighs us down, not just as individuals, but as communities and societies, in our common quest to find and fill our true potential."
—Bob Graham, former governor of Florida and
United States senator

"Gail Blanke's THROW OUT FIFTY THINGS is the perfect road map to help you lighten your load. Leave it to a friend like Gail—wise, funny, practical, and so very organized—to empty my closets and clean out my shelves, while soothing the spirit and soul, too. This book is a keeper."
—Linda Fairstein, bestselling author of *Lethal Legacy*

"THROW OUT FIFTY THINGS is a refreshing book full of practical tips and helpful insights. The title is the simple principle. Applied at home, in your career, in your mind, or in your business, it helps you get rid of the clutter that blocks success. Perhaps most astounding is how relevant the insights are to leading a business today."
—Peter Loescher, President & CEO of Siemens AG

"Gail Blanke is a motivator and a liberator. THROW OUT FIFTY THINGS is certain to be a classic, especially for those seeking a simpler, more meaningful way of life."
—Beth Comstock, Chief Marketing Officer,
The General Electric Company

Throw Out Fifty Things

Clear the Clutter, Find Your Life

⁛

GAIL BLANKE

SPRINGBOARD PRESS

NEW YORK   BOSTON

The individuals who have been identified in this book by first and last name have granted me permission to use their real names. The individuals who have only been identified using a first name are based on real people or composites drawn from my work as a life coach. I have changed the names of those individuals and modified personally identifiable details.

Parts of Chapters 14, 15, 17, 18, 23, and 24 were originally published in *Real Simple* magazine in a slightly modified form.

Springboard Press
Hachette Book Group
237 Park Avenue, New York, NY 10017
Visit our Web site at www.HachetteBookGroup.com

First Edition: March 2009

Springboard Press is an imprint of Grand Central Publishing. The Springboard name and logo are trademarks of Hachette Book Group.

Library of Congress Cataloging-in-Publication Data
Blanke, Gail.
    Throw out fifty things : clear the clutter, find your life / Gail Blanke. — 1st ed.
        p. cm.
    "Gail Blanke offers inspiring ways to clear away the debris of your life—both physical and mental—to help you find peace, energy, and a better vision of who you are."—Provided by the publisher.
    ISBN-13: 978-0-446-50579-6
    ISBN-10: 0-446-50579-X
    1. House cleaning. 2. Orderliness. 3. Storage in the home.
4. Selp-help techniques. I. Title. II. Title: Throw out 50 things.
    TX324.B53 2009
    648'.5—dc22   2008029908

10 9 8 7 6 5 4

Printed in the United States of America

For Jim

Acknowledgments

✣

The truth is, this book wouldn't have been possible if my mom hadn't threatened to turn all my dresser drawers upside down and told me to "Get crackin' and throw out all that junk, and I mean *now!*" that summer day when I was fourteen. And it wouldn't have been possible if my dad hadn't told me to "Get rid of anything that drags you down, sweetie. Moving through a bunch of negative clutter is like walking underwater. It's hard to get where you want to go." I sure was a lucky kid.

Look, I didn't come by this "throwing out" thing naturally, in spite of my otherwise pretty good genes. I had to acquire a passion for letting go, throwing out, and pressing the "delete" button in more than a few areas of my life. Chances are, if you've picked up this book, you aren't exactly the oracle of organization or the diva of decluttering either. But you've got a longing—okay, maybe not yet a passion—to clear the decks so *you* can "get crackin'" with the next segment of your life.

And the people you'll meet inside these pages have that

same longing, too. And they also have something else that you have: courage. It takes courage to let go of the past. It takes courage to actually make a decision to throw something—anything—out. As you'll see, for many of the men and women who have been generous enough to share their stories, actually throwing out fifty things wasn't always (frequently, but not always) a laugh a minute. But they found the courage to do it anyway. And in some cases, it changed their lives. It'll change yours, too.

In particular, I'm indebted to Laurel Bernstein, Jane Blecher, Dan Blodgett, Eddie Brill, Sally Carr, Beth Comstock, Lue Ann Eldar, David Evangelista, Martha Gilliland, David Hoffman, Phil Hough, Parvin Klein, Alan Matarasso, Marychris Melli, Patricia and Roger Miller, David Molko, Pat Perkins, Richard Pine, Scott Preiss, Kathy Robb, and Ray Sclafani.

Richard Pine, my dear friend and literary agent, kept me motivated throughout the entire process of putting this book together. "Just keep writing, Gail," was his daily dictum. It worked. And Karen Murgolo is simply the world's best and most supportive editor. In fact her whole team is terrific: Matthew Ballast and Erica Gelbard are superb publicists, while Tom Hardej became, among other things, my "organizational muse." And Laura Jorstad, in my view, is the queen of copy editing. And anyone who's ever called or come to my office knows my indomitable former assistant, Jane Blecher, stand-up comic, resident pharmacologist, and one-of-a-kind friend. But most of all, I'm grateful beyond words to Jim, Kate, and Abigail, the best family any gal ever had. Ever.

We are all passionate pilgrims on the road to an uncertain but glorious future, *shedding as we go* everything that's a drag, and anything that causes us to pause, second-guess ourselves, or—heaven forbid—turn around and go back.

I'm really glad you're with us.

Contents

⁙

Introduction   xv

Fueling the Urge to Purge   xxii

Making It to Fifty   xxiv

Getting Started   xxvi

PART ONE: Getting Rid of the Physical Stuff

Chapter 1   Your Bedroom   3

Chapter 2   Your Bathroom   17

Chapter 3   Your Kitchen   28

Chapter 4   Your Living Room   40

Chapter 5   Your Dining Room   50

Chapter 6   Your Attic   58

Chapter 7   Your Garage   69

PART TWO: Your Office: Paring Down the
                Professional Clutter

Chapter 8   Clarifying Your Brand   85

Chapter 9   Keeping What Works, Eliminating
What Doesn't   97

Chapter 10   The Phoenix Rises from the Ashes   107

PART THREE: Attacking the Mental Mess

If You Think You Can Separate the Physical from the
Mental Clutter, Forget About It!   112

Chapter 11   Letting Go of Feeling Inadequate, Irrelevant,
and Just Plain Not Good Enough   119

Chapter 12   Letting Go of the Type of Person You
Think You Are—or Aren't   127

Chapter 13   Letting Go of the Regrets and
Mistakes of the Past   137

Chapter 14   Letting Go of Being Right About How
Wrong Everybody and Everything Is   148

Chapter 15   Letting Go of the Need to Have
Everyone Like You   159

Chapter 16   Letting Go of Thinking the Worst   169

Chapter 17   Letting Go of Waiting for the
Right Moment   181

Chapter 18   Letting Go of Needing to Feel Secure   190

Chapter 19   Letting Go of Thinking That You Have
to Do Everything Yourself   197

Chapter 20   Making It to Fifty: The Celebration   208

PART FOUR: Stepping into the Clearing

Chapter 21   Your Vision for the Future   213

Chapter 22   Taking Energy from Your Defining
Moments   223

Chapter 23   Being Unforgettable   232

Chapter 24   Find Your Song—and Sing It!   241

Chapter 25   Your Declaration to the World   248

Appendix: Your Throw-Outs   249

Resource Guide   253

Index   261

Introduction

✣

Whenever people ask me to describe my coaching "methodology," I tell them I use the Michelangelo Method. Inevitably, especially if they're human resources people, they look puzzled and say, "What the heck is that? I never heard of it." And I always respond with, "Of course you have. You remember that wonderful story of Michelangelo who, shortly after he'd finished sculpting the statue of David, was asked by a local patron of the arts who had been completely awestruck after first viewing the statue, 'How did you know to sculpt David? I just don't understand . . .' And Michelangelo, being a straightforward, honest sort of fellow, allegedly responded, 'Oh, well, David was always there in the marble. I just took away everything that was not David."

And that's my job as your coach: to help you *let go* of all the extraneous marble; to chisel your way through the stuff, junk, and clutter—physical and mental—that stands in the way of helping your very best self move into the next glorious phase of your life.

Our lives are so filled with the debris of the past—from dried-up tubes of Krazy Glue to old grudges—that it's a wonder we can get up in the morning, never mind go to work, care for our children and parents, and just put one foot in front of the other. And living in the Information Age doesn't help, either. We're constantly bombarded from every direction by flying debris in another form: the news, the media. On television, on the radio, on our cell phones, online, and in the air, we're deluged with what too often turns out to be life marble—*garbage* might be a better word: all the stuff that's gone wrong in the world, gone wrong in ourselves, gone wrong in our lives. Or could go wrong. Oh, I'm not saying we don't need to be informed. We do. We're citizens of a planet on the move, and we must know what needs to be done to keep it spinning forward. But we can't move forward, we can't move at all, if we're locked inside a block of marble, largely of our own making.

So what can we do? It's time to chisel our way out, to blast through the stuff we've heaped upon ourselves, and step out into the clearing. It's time. Now. I'm not kidding. The arteries of our lives are blocked, and that blockage threatens our ability to be happy, to make others happy, and to play our part in moving humankind forward.

Look, I come by this urge to let go and to urge others to let go naturally: My mother was a Virgo. You should have seen her drawers. If she asked you to get something for her, she'd say, "It's in my bureau in the third drawer on the left on the right-hand side, in the back on the very bottom of the stack."

And she'd be absolutely right. I'm an Aquarian. Oh, I'm not saying we're the slobs of the Zodiac—I mean, I put things away in my drawers—I just don't always know what things are in which drawers. And if you're a certain sign, does that mean you're going to have messy drawers? Maybe. Anyway, once when I was about thirteen years old, my mother threatened to turn all of my drawers upside down on the floor of my bedroom to teach me to finally get them organized. Thankfully, she didn't actually do it. (And unfortunately, my drawers will never hold a candle to hers.) But one thing she was able to teach me was to *throw things out.*

"If you don't know what to do with it, or where to put it or why you ever bought it in the first place, or if looking at it depresses you, throw it out!" she'd say. "Never keep anything that makes you *look* heavy or *feel* heavy."

As it turns out, my mom was right about a lot of stuff, and the throwing-things-out rule was one of her best. Oh, and whenever she asked any of us to throw things out, she meant for us to do it *now, not later.* We called it her *Do it now or oh, brother!* mood.

So it's not surprising that when I coach people, I always ask them to throw things out. And not just a few things; I ask everyone I work with, at the end of our second or third session, to go home and throw out fifty things. "And by the way"—I usually look stern here—"magazines and catalogs only count as one thing. You can throw out a hundred of them, but they only count as one." People usually look at me with both horror and annoyance. (But go ahead and throw out fifty things anyway—you'll feel like a million bucks.) "Look," they'll say, "I just went through my closets and I've already thrown out everything I can. Forget it."

But I don't forget it. Just like my mother didn't. And not only do I ask them to throw out fifty things, I ask them to make a list of what they're throwing out. Actually, it's not that hard to get into the swing of it. Look, you've had that single earring for years and you keep hoping the other one will show up. It won't. Throw it away. You've got all those socks with no matches. (I know, they were in pairs when you put them in the dryer. I've always wondered what happens to them. Do they pop up in someone else's dryer? I don't know.) Throw them out. You've got that single leather glove but you think it's not right to throw away a leather glove; it's okay, throw it away. You've got all that makeup from your old look. Toss it. And you've got that drawer in the kitchen. You know that drawer. There are receipts in there from years ago, there's a bunch of change in there, and, yes, there are old dried-up tubes of Krazy Glue. And you know what else is in there? Keys. There are keys in there that haven't opened up anything in decades. But you think it's not nice to throw away keys. They're heavy and make a clanking noise when they hit the bottom of the wastebasket. Never mind. Throw them out. Throw it all out.

Here's why: Once you start throwing out a lot of physical clutter—once you get on a roll, and you will—a new urge kicks in: "What about all the clutter in my *mind*?" you ask. "What in the world have I allowed to collect there?" And then you get into the really good stuff.

Of course it's the mental clutter that drags you down and holds you back, that keeps you from stepping into the next great segment of your life—the one that's filled with promise, joy, adventure, and best of all fulfillment. *You can't move forward into the future when you're constantly sucked back into the past.* So in addition to the socks and lipsticks, you're going to throw out the old regrets and resentments, the resignation, the fear of failing or the fear of succeeding; you're going to let go of the times when you came up a little bit short (we all have them). And you're going to let go of the *voices* that remind you of your so-called limitations. You know those voices. Just when you're feeling pretty spunky and sure of yourself—just when you've created a bold new vision for your life—that voice from the past says, "Not so fast, kiddo, you can't do that! You don't have enough time, you don't have enough energy, you don't have enough money, and anyway, *they'll* never let you!"

A word about the voices: Whenever you're out for something big, whenever you're stepping out of your comfort zone and into your power, you'll hear them. It's inevitable. And it's okay. In fact, I'd suggest that if you go along for months and don't hear any voices, chances are you're playing it too safe. Chances are, you're hanging out in the stands when you should be strutting onto the field. The minute you enter the game, you'll hear the voices. Congratulate yourself and say, "I must be about to live up to my potential. Let 'er rip!"

One *more* word about voices: Did you see the movie *A Beautiful Mind*? If you did, you'll remember that the main protagonist is John Nash, the brilliant and world-renowned mathematician and co-recipient of the 1994 Nobel Prize in Economics, played by Russell Crowe. Nash suffered from severe paranoid schizophrenia, to the point that he saw and heard imaginary people who interacted intimately with him and negatively influenced his life—almost ruining his career and marriage, even endangering the lives of the people he loved. Toward the end of the film, Nash is teaching at Princeton where he'd done his undergraduate work. A fellow from the Nobel Prize committee comes to have tea with him and to, unofficially, determine if Nash is more or less "fit enough" to receive the prize. He asks Nash, "So, do you still um, you know, uh . . ." Nash finishes his sentence, "See them? Yes, they're still there. But I choose not to acknowledge them . . . That's what it's like with all our dreams and all our nightmares. You've got to keep feeding them for them to stay alive." I figure that if on any given day, John Nash can see and hear those torturous people who attempt to derail his life, but choose not to acknowledge them—then we can, too. We can say to ourselves when those negative, Not-so-fast, Who-do-you-think-you-are?, Let's-not-get-carried-away voices flood our minds: "Not today. I'm not listening today. I have my own hill to take, my own rivers to cross. Not today."

Here's a good story: A woman came into my office not long ago with what was supposed to be her list of throwaways but didn't want to talk about it. She had taken a leaf out of John Nash's playbook and was focused on what was important to her—and only on what was important to her. When she'd left my office a couple of weeks earlier, she'd been resolute about letting go of whatever was dragging her down or holding her back. At the time, I didn't know how resolute.

"C'mon," I said. "What are you throwing out?"

Finally she said, "Okay, okay, I'll tell you. I went home after our last session and threw out the guy I'd been living with for eleven years! I finally realized he was the one who was holding me back and weighing me down.

"But Gail," she continued, looking worried, "do I still have to throw out forty-nine more things?"

"That'll do it for today," I said. "Take the week off. Then you can get crackin' on the next forty-nine!"

Okay, now it's your turn. This is the beginning of the Big Letting-Go.

Fueling the Urge to Purge

Do you ever notice how much lighter you feel when you clean out your closet in the spring? And depending on how packed, cluttered, and bursting at the seams it was, you might feel positively ebullient. Not to mention proud. "Hey, you want to see my closet?" is a question I've asked various hapless members of my family if they've wandered too close after the urge to purge has had its way with me.

Personally, I don't think we pay enough attention to the lighter, prouder feeling that comes from cleaning stuff out of our lives. We acknowledge ourselves only momentarily; we don't celebrate our accomplishment or the lighter spirit that comes with it. And unfortunately, we don't marshal the force of that new, light spirit to propel us forward. But we could. We could purge ourselves of life plaque on a regular basis and use the accompanying power surges to get whatever we want in life.

So let's do that. Let's decide now that we're going to start a new monthly, weekly, or even daily ritual of throwing things out and letting things go—and that we're going to invite all the people we care about to join us. Can you imagine the collective energy we'll unleash? The positive power surge we'll create? We could change the world.

The Rules of Disengagement

How do you know what to throw out? Well, luckily, the rules of disengagement are really simple:

- **One.** If *it*—the thing, the belief or conviction, the memory, the job, even the person—weighs you down, clogs you up, or just plain makes you feel bad about yourself, throw it out, give it away, sell it, let it go, move on.
- **Two.** If it (see above!) just sits there, taking up room and contributing nothing positive to your life, throw it out, give it away, sell it, let it go, move on. If you're not moving forward, you're moving backward. Throwing out what's negative helps you rediscover what's positive.
- **Three.** Don't make the decision—whether to toss it or keep it—a hard one. If you have to weigh the pros and cons for too long or agonize about the right thing to do, throw it out.
- **Four.** Don't be afraid. This is your life we're talking about. The only one you've got for sure. You don't have the time, energy, or room for physical or psychic waste.

Making It to Fifty

You're really going to be surprised by how easy it is to throw out fifty things. And I have to say here and now that the reason for fifty is not arbitrary. Once you make it to fifty, a kind of wonderful momentum takes over; before you know it, the throwing-out thing becomes a habit, an ongoing mind-set. And then something really, really good happens: You take control of your life. You start living it, it stops living you. Did you ever see or read Eugene Ionesco's play *The Chairs*? Well, if you did, you'll remember that the last scene shows a bunch of chairs on the stage. That's it, just chairs. No people. That's because the point Ionesco's making is that in the end, if we're not paying attention, the stuff in our lives owns us. We don't own it. And it endures; we don't.

But we're not going to let that happen.

And to make it really easy for you, this book is divided into four parts:

In part 1, "Getting Rid of the Physical Stuff," you and I make our way through the major areas of your house and mine—from that good ol' kitchen drawer to the medicine cabinet to the far corners of the attic—and together we muster the courage to let go of the stuff that clogs our life arteries, weighs us down, or simply doesn't serve us anymore. And just for the record, we mean to be "green" in this heroic effort—as you'll see.

In part 2, "Your Office: Paring Down the Professional Clutter," we move into the office—whether it's in some towering skyscraper or in a small nook in your bedroom—and throw out the debris that's accumulated there, which just might be slowing down your ability to gain traction in a new assignment, a new company, or even a whole new career.

In part 3, "Attacking the Mental Mess," we go after the really good stuff. Because once you're warmed up from tossing out all your physical clutter, you can have a field day with your mental and emotional debris. And you're going to be surprised at what a lot of useless junk you've allowed to collect in your head. And, you'll be even more surprised by how lighthearted and even light-headed you'll feel when you throw *that* stuff out. At the end of this section, my friend, you'll have made it to fifty. Actually, I have the feeling you'll have made it *way past* fifty—and it'll be time to celebrate.

Then, in part 4, "Stepping into the Clearing," *we clarify the essential you.* This is where you decide who you are at the core, what your own idea of *good* is—and how you want to live the next great segment of your life. And this is where you find the stuff to step forward with grace and confidence. This is where you learn to be nothing short of unforgettable.

To help you keep careful track of all your throw-outs, you can use the template provided at the back of this book as well as the running scorecard at the end of each chapter. You can also log on to www.throwoutfiftythings .com and download the *Throw Out Fifty Things* workbook. Once you've hit fifty, come online and post your list of throw-outs, okay? I bet you'll have some great stories to tell us. And sharing them will motivate others to start *their* own throwing-out process. Then they'll encourage someone else, and before you know it we'll have created a Throw Out Fifty Things *Movement.* Let's do it.

So get out your workbooks or your pads of paper, we're moving into your bedroom . . . right after we assemble a few items that are going to make this whole process a piece of cake.

"But Gail," you're probably saying, "how long do I have?"

Two weeks, my friend. And that's plenty long enough. I'm not kidding.

Getting Started

Before you move into that bedroom, collect the following things. (You probably have these at home.)

- Sturdy garbage bags (get the kind you can't see through, so that once you have put your giveaways in them, you can't see them anymore). Cardboard boxes work, too, if you happen to have some stacked from deliveries or a recent move.
- A pad of medium-size sticky notes, to label your bags.
- A waterproof marker to write on the sticky notes.
- A box of gallon-size ziplock bags, to store single

> items for giving away, and for small items like jewelry.
> - Masking tape, to secure the boxes or bags, mend tears in the bags, and secure the notes to the bags or boxes.

Bring these items with you from room to room as you throw things out.

Start with three big bags. Make one TRASH. Get that marker out, write TRASH on one of the sticky notes, and stick it onto a bag. Now, how hard was that? You already have trash going! Items that are ripped, torn, badly stained, or truly unusable because they're broken or parts are missing go into the TRASH bag. This bag is definitely going out with the trash.

Make the next bag DONATIONS. Add a similar note to this second bag. Note that mismatched pairs—socks, gloves—are accepted at homeless shelters, where they will be paired and distributed.

Write SELL on the sticky note for the third bag. Here's where you'll put all those things that you'd like to include in a tag or garage sale, or send to a consignment or resale store. Oh, and if you're in need of cleaning rags, you can always start a fourth bag for all the lonely socks, torn towels, or worn bedding. At our house, we use the torn towels for the dog on rainy days.

Now you're ready to dig in.

❖

PART ONE

Getting Rid of
the Physical Stuff

| Chapter 1 | Your Bedroom |

Okay, let's remember the Rules of Disengagement: If *it*—the article of clothing, the shoes, the lamp, whatever—weighs you down or makes you feel bad about yourself, or if it just sits there taking up room and contributing nothing positive, it goes out. If you find you're spending a lot of time trying to figure out whether or not to keep it or toss it, *it* goes out. And finally, *don't be afraid.* This is your life we're talking about, and we're going let go of anything that clutters it up. Starting now.

Okay, it's always easier to start with the low-hanging fruit. Just walk into your bedroom and look around. What do you see? How do you feel? Are you glad to be there; do you feel relaxed, serene, even clearheaded? I don't, at least not as much as I'd like to.

I'll tell you what I see: I see decorative pillows from five years ago that really depress me. I don't know how to explain it, but they're too dark and ornate for what I want to be a light, airy room. And two of them are slightly chewed at the corners thanks to our ten-month-old golden retriever. (Her name's Willa and if I threw out all the stuff she's gnawed I could easily get to fifty things . . . but there might not be much left.) Anyway, those pillows are going. (Remember, groups of things, for the most part, only count as one, so although I'm throwing out five depressing pillows I can only put down a "one" next to them.) They're going into one of those big black Hefty bags labeled DONATIONS, and eventually I'll give them to Goodwill or the Salvation Army. It would be easy to put them in the attic or the back of my husband's closet (he'd never notice them, believe me), but they'd still be here and that just doesn't walk the dog. We're talking about *throwing stuff out,* not moving it around.

So let's open our first drawer. Everything okay in there? Are there socks that don't match? What about all the single gloves—are you going to wear two different-colored right-handed gloves or wait another couple of years for their mates to show up? And what about the too-small sweaters that your sister-in-law keeps giving you Christmas after Christmas? She won't really know that you threw them out, and actually you'll give them away. They're perfectly good sweaters, just not for you. And how about that T-shirt from the old company outing you dragged yourself to (you referred to it as "forced fun," remember?) two weeks before you and your entire department were so unceremoniously eliminated? It really has to go. It's no longer worthy of your wearing it—even just to jog in—seriously. Because every time you put it on it's going to make you feel that somehow the firings were your fault, that you should have done something differently, that maybe you're not all that good and you somehow deserved to be downsized. Sounds ridiculous, I know, but that's what we do: If something goes wrong, we make it all about us. Too bad we don't do that when something goes right! You get the picture. The T-shirt goes out. And the *shoulds* go with it. Throw them out.

While we're in our drawers, let's consider my dear friend Barbara Brennan's throw-out technique, which she refers to as "periodic purges." "I grew up with piles," she says, "so I feel oddly comfortable having piles around. That is, as long as I know what's in the pile."

I like the idea of being "oddly comfortable" with piles. It's good to know what you're okay with and what drives you crazy, and not buy into someone else's idea of the neatness imperative, don't you think?

"But I live in a cozy New York apartment," Barbara continues. "*Cozy* is a code word for 'limited closet space,' so I can't let the piles get too high." The way Barbara keeps from being overrun by her stuff, not to mention her piles, is by taking it one drawer or shelf at a time. "Every month or so, I do an area cleanout. Maybe I tackle a jewelry drawer or a shelf in my closet. Nothing overwhelming, nothing too time consuming. But I always feel better, lighter, and more clearly focused, not to mention extremely pleased with myself." I like her attitude: Do it, but don't make it a big deal.

Speaking of a jewelry drawer, I bet you have one where you keep all your costume jewelry. I do and it's a real mess.

I used to work at Avon, and I received new pieces of jewelry every two weeks that were featured in each new Avon brochure. Wait a minute, where did all these giant metal earrings come from? I must've looked like a freak wearing them. Still, they weren't all that cheap and they do have a certain charm to them. Sort of. I can't just throw them in the wastebasket. They'd clank when they hit bottom. I hate that. But I'm done with that old look so what am I hanging on to this stuff for? I'll put them (five pairs, but one "thing") in a small ziplock bag and keep them with the stuff for Goodwill or maybe for someone I know who might appreciate them. Actually, the young daughter of a friend of mine might like them for playing dress-up. Are you going to throw out those old beads from that trip to Jamaica? Go ahead. At least give them away. You haven't worn them in over four years and someone else might be absolutely delighted by them. How many things have we got so far? I've got three and you've got three, too. We're not doing badly.

Listen, as you're rummaging through your stuff, keep your eye out for things that you might be done with but that could absolutely delight someone else.

Here's a great story that illustrates my point: Several years ago, we were conducting a Lifedesigns workshop for working women to help them create not only successful, enriching careers, but also happy, fulfilled lives. On the first day of the workshop, we were discussing various things in our lives that had caused us to be angry or disappointed; things or events that we'd like to get over. One woman,

Carrie, talked about how disappointed she'd been on her tenth birthday when she failed to get her heart's desire: one of those expandable heart bracelets that were all the rage among little girls decades ago. What made it worse was that her cousin, who lived with her family, had celebrated her birthday the following week and *she* got the bracelet. Carrie was hurt, jealous, and furious at her cousin. In fact she held that birthday against her for decades, somehow blaming her for having been given the bracelet she'd wanted so much. "I know it sounds funny, but I still haven't quite gotten over it," said Carrie, who was now forty-seven years old.

Well, that afternoon I asked the participants, as I always do at the end of the first day, to go home and throw out fifty things and be ready to report back the following morning to the other women. Another participant, Mary Beth, turned up early with a big grin on her face. "Guess what I found," she said, beaming. "An expandable heart bracelet! It was at the bottom of my junk drawer in my bedroom. Let's give it to Carrie!" Well, not only did we give it to her, but we gift-wrapped the bracelet, bought a small cake with ten candles on it, and sang "Happy Tenth Birthday, Dear Carrie" at the tops of our lungs. She was knocked out, of course, and very moved. We all were. Then Carrie put on the heart bracelet and went outside to call her cousin and tell her how much she loved her.

Let's move into our closets. I don't know how it happened, but my closet has gotten considerably more crowded and messy during the last year. I'd like to blame it on the fact that I've been really busy, or maybe on the fact that the seasons are all messed up in New York and I've needed lighter-weight clothes in the winter and heavier clothes in the summer so that's why they're all crammed in there together. Or it could be because my daughters, Kate and Abigail, and I share some of the same clothes from time to time, and somehow they all end up in my closet. We all wear the same size shoe (which is good) and we all share a shoe fetish (which is bad), so the floor of my closet is a repository for whatever shoes they're not particularly interested in at the moment—but I'm allowed to borrow. Actually, none of these excuses is valid.

The real reasons my closet is a mess are: (a) I could never make it as neat as my mother's so why try; and (b) sorting things out and throwing things away involves making decisions. And making decisions can be an exhausting process.

Green Tip: Recycle Your Sneakers

Did you know that you can actually recycle your old athletic shoes? Nike has a program called Reuse-A-Shoe (www.letmeplay.com/reuseashoe) in which the company collects worn-out sneakers of any brand and then processes and recycles them into materials for playgrounds and athletic courts.

You know, I've got to figure out what's important, what's not; what I really need, what I don't; what might come back into fashion, what won't in a million years; what really looks good on me whether it's in fashion or not, what looked wrong from the beginning; what makes me feel heavy physically or emotionally; what makes me feel light and upbeat; what's me, what's not. I could get exhausted thinking about it. And look, it's always easier not to decide. That way you leave all your options open, right? Deciding not to decide, or deciding to decide later, is *hoshmahoken* (a word my parents and their friends in Cleveland made up as a substitute for, well, I guess, *BS*). Not deciding is the number one cause of *all* the clutter—physical, emotional, and spiritual—in our lives. And if we can't decide what to throw out of our clothes closets, how in the world are we going to decide what to throw out of our mental closets—closets that are overflowing with the debris of indecisions? This thought alone gives new meaning to the term *mind boggling,* doesn't it? But we don't have to be seduced by the appeal of not deciding—we can grit our overly whitened teeth and just do it. I can tell you my mom didn't spend a lot of time weighing the pros and cons of what to keep and what to discard. She decided and that was it. Smart people make things hard. Brilliant people make things easy. My mom was brilliant. Okay, my closet, not to mention my drawers, will never look like hers. It's okay. I bet somehow it's even okay with her. I'll do it my way.

So once again, here we are in the closet. And it's no accident that we're standing here together gathering up our strength to actually decide who we are, or who we could be, based on what we keep in here. Get out the cardboard boxes and Hefty bags, ziplock bags and sticky notes. Keep them open and handy. Smile as you fill them up.

I'm definitely deciding to throw out three suits I see hanging here. I haven't worn them for at least seven years. They're still in good shape, but they're just no longer me. I've been dressing slightly less corporate since I started my own business ten years ago; I have more fun and am much more creative with my outfits—and my clients seem to get a kick out of it. So these stiff suits go out.

Swap Your Clothes

Another great way to get rid of the clothes from your old look is to hold a swap party. Send invitations to all your friends and ask them to bring the clothes they're ready to toss, too. Serve food and drinks and make it a true party. You can even set up mirrors or a small runway so everyone can show off their new looks. If all goes according to plan, each of your friends will leave with something new that complements her style and makes her feel good about herself . . . even a heart bracelet!

A wonderful and very funny woman I know named Tara took the closet decision very seriously. In fact, she took it to the ultimate. She threw out everything and I mean *everything.* She threw out every article of clothing she had: from evening gowns to jogging shorts, from flip-flops to Pradas, from suits for working to suits for swimming. She even threw out all her underwear and lingerie. Everything. Well, not everything. She kept a beautiful suit that her mother had given her years earlier to celebrate her first "real" job. It didn't fit anymore and it wasn't in vogue, but it represented a milestone in her life—one that was worth re-celebrating from time to time. It's interesting to note what we keep as well as what we throw out, isn't it? The point is to have a reason for both—keeping and throwing out. That's where the *deciding* comes in.

Remember, if it makes you feel bad, it doesn't add anything to your life, or you have to agonize over your decision too long, let it go. If, on the other hand, it makes you feel good just to have it; if there's a positive emotional attachment to it, regardless of whether or not you'll ever "use" it again: Keep it. **Our aim is not to create a merely tidy or well-organized life. Our aim is to clarify who we are now, to *decide* what's important to us now, and to answer the question, What the heck am I doing here?**

In the case of Tara, she threw out all her clothes (except for the "special suit") because she wanted to entirely reinvent herself and she decided, rightfully, that if she changed the way she looked, the way she adorned her body, it would help her think of herself differently. "I'm done with the old me," she said. "I feel like I'm coming out of a cocoon." It's true, the new Tara was ready to emerge. Not all of us are in a position financially, or even emotionally, to go to the extreme Tara did. But you've got to admit it's impressive and even inspiring for the rest of us. Eventually, she even changed her hair color and style, lost weight, worked out, and developed a totally toned-up persona.

How many things have we thrown out so far? By my count I've got in the neighborhood of three, since all the pillows only count as one, and so do the suits and the jewelry. You might have more, though, depending on how you did with your socks, gloves, and jewelry. See? This isn't all that hard, is it? Well, okay, some of it is. But a lot of it's wonderful.

A man I know who was committed to making it to fifty was going through his closet looking for throw-outs when he came upon a beat-up envelope that had been shoved inside an old shoe box. His name, MICHAEL, was handwritten on the front. There was no address, so it must have been delivered by hand. He'd forgotten all about the envelope, and in fact he'd never opened it. He couldn't even remember who had given it to him or under what circumstances. He was about to toss it into the wastebasket but then, on a whim, he decided to open it. Inside was a piece of yellow, lined paper with writing on both sides. He looked at the signature: "Justine." *Justine?* he thought. *Who in the world . . . wait, wasn't that that very smart girl in my class at business school? Yes! She was the one who helped me with statistics. If it weren't for her, I'd never have . . .* He started to read the letter and immediately started to kick himself for somehow stashing it away, unread, fifteen years ago.

"Dear Michael," Justine had written, "Now that we're graduating and will probably never see each other again, I've finally gotten up the courage to tell you what I meant to tell you a million times when we were working together. I'm in love with you . . ." Michael was dumbfounded. He'd thought of Justine as his tutor and friend. Never as a potential girlfriend. (Michael had dated just one girl all the way through college and graduate school and eventually married her—and, unfortunately, divorced her.) Justine went on to explain that she knew he was very much involved with someone else and that there was no chance of their ever getting together but that nevertheless, she wanted him to know how she felt, that he was, in her mind, the most wonderful, talented person she'd ever met—and that it had been an absolute joy working with him. She wished him all the very best. She wouldn't forget him.

Well, you know what happened next. Michael, thanks to the wonders of Google, located Justine. She was working in an investment banking firm in New York (Michael lived in LA), and according to the Google data she just might not be married—at least not at the moment. He called her up and told her about finding the letter and how sorry he was not to have opened it fifteen years sooner.

They decided to meet for dinner in New York (sounds like *An Affair to Remember*, right?) and, yes, it was nothing short of kismet. They've been having an incredibly happy relationship for nearly a year now. Who knows where it will lead? Someplace good, I bet.

When You Can't Do It Alone

If you're more like me (and less like my mom) and just can't seem to get your closet organized, did you know that you can hire someone to help? If you can't afford a professional closet organizer, like California Closets, the Container Store also offers a service where they will take a look at your closet, make a plan with you, and help you pick out the various products you'll need to sort things out.

So dig around in that closet of yours, okay? Out of the clutter and chaos could come, well, something or someone you've been looking for.

Steps for clearing the clutter in your bedroom:

1. Walk into your bedroom as if for the first time. How does it make you feel? Is it the kind of room that could help restore you at the end of a frenetic

day? What furniture, decorations, knickknacks, or just plain junk do you see that would hamper a feeling of calm? Gather it up; get rid of it.

2. Walk into your closet and open all your drawers. Examine the clothes, shoes, and accessories you find there. Will it make you feel good when you think of putting them on—or do some of these items give you a heavy, slightly depressed feeling and drag you back into the past? The things that make you feel heavy—physically or emotionally—have to go. Look, we can't all buy a totally new wardrobe all at once, but we can gradually edit out the stuff that weighs us down.

3. Ask yourself these questions: Who am I now and what am I becoming? Do my clothes, does this very important room, represent the way I'd like to think of myself? What has to change to make that happen? You don't have to change everything all at once, but you do have to start now.

4. Make a neat pile of the clothing; put old jewelry and accessories into boxes; gather up the decorative items that no longer fit; and label each container with the sticky notes and waterproof pen. Use a bag for the shoes and label them in terms of where they're going—in the trash or to Goodwill or to be recycled. (See the resource guide at the end of this book.)

Gail's Throw-Out Scorecard:

> 5 decorative pillows
>
> 3 old corporate suits
>
> 6 pairs of shoes
>
> **Total: 3 things**

Your Throw-Out Scorecard:

_____

_____

_____

_____

_____

_____

Your Total:

Chapter 2 | **Your Bathroom**

Let's move into your bathroom. There are a lot of throw-out candidates in there. Take a look at your medicine cabinet. I'm looking at mine and I'm embarrassed to say that there are *very* old containers and tubes of over-the-counter drugs—some of them are actually dried out or with expiration dates that have long passed. And there are prescription drugs from more than five years ago. I've read that they lose their potency and effectiveness after a certain period of time. Whether that's true or not, it doesn't seem healthful—physically or mentally—to keep old drugs for old ailments, or even potentially new ailments. I'm a great proponent of the Mind Over Matter philosophy. In fact, I wholeheartedly believe that *we are what we think about,* which I'll talk a lot more about later. Suffice it to say, surrounding ourselves with a lot of old medicines is negative, robs energy, and may even warm the way for those old ailments to remake their homes in our bodies.

So what are we deciding here? That we might get sick

and need these old, expired drugs, or that we *intend to be well* and not need them again? Tiger Woods was interviewed right before a recent National Open at the Oakmont Country Club outside Pittsburgh. The reporter asked him why he wasn't practicing getting out of the "Church Pews"—the course's infamous bunkers, so deep and so treacherous that they had wrecked the games of many a would-be championship golfer. Tiger's reply was simple: "Because I don't intend to get in them."

Don't Let Your Expired Medication Leak into the Food Chain

The old method of getting rid of expired medications was to flush the pills down the toilet, but it's now been shown that traces of such medicines can show up in our water supplies. And if you simply throw them in the trash, they could leak into the soil. So how do you get rid of them? Check your local pharmacy; they may collect expired drugs. You can let the experts dispose of them properly!

We underestimate the power of our intentions. If we actually *intend* to be well, then right here, right now we have to decide what we're going to do to create that reality. For example, does this mean that we're definitely going to move more and eat less? (You can complicate the diet/fitness thing if you want to. There are about a zillion books on the subject out there for you to read, and given their reported sales figures, chances are you've read, or at least bought, a few of them. But basically, it comes down pretty much to how much you move versus how much you eat, and you and I both know it.) Does this also mean we're going to eat fewer carbs, trans fats, and red meat, and more fruits and vegetables? Does it possibly mean that you intend—and will do *whatever it takes*—to stop smoking rather than just "try"? Am I getting carried away? (My mother always said I shouldn't get carried away but I don't care. And sometimes, getting carried away is good. Like now.) Look, it all comes down to what you're throwing out, doesn't it?

These are some big questions to tackle while we're standing here in the bathroom. (And you thought you were just going to throw out a bunch of stuff.) So what'll it be? Do these old prescription drugs and other old medications go or do they stay? The great news is: *You* get to decide. I'm deciding to throw this old stuff out.

I used to get really severe migraines. I've been in more emergency wards in more hospitals across the country than I can shake a stick at. But I haven't had a really paralyzing migraine in about ten years. Still, here in my medicine chest is a packet of the heavy-duty medication I used to take to put me to sleep and do heaven knows what else, until a day or two passed and the headache went away. I'm throwing it out. I'm not going to be held hostage by the fear of an old pain that I don't intend to have ever again. I feel better already. But this is important: Next to your column titled BATHROOM THROWAWAYS, make a column called BATHROOM *MENTAL* THROWAWAYS, okay? Write down any negative assumptions you made about your health and well-being that you want to let go of. Replace your intention to be sick with your intention to be well.

Here's the biggest one for me: Nearly two years ago, I had "surprise" double bypass surgery. It was a surprise because I'd always been in perfect health, never smoked, followed a healthy diet, worked out daily, and had perfect EKGs, clear chest X-rays, and low blood pressure. Quite frankly, if I hadn't followed my instincts that told me something was wrong despite various doctors insisting I was one of the healthiest people they'd ever met, I might not be here today. But I got through the surgery with flying colors. Like all heart patients, I was given a little plastic blower that I was instructed to use every hour to help clear my lungs. I was pretty good about using it, and finally my lungs were pronounced clear as a bell. That blower is right there in my bathroom closet. I'm going to throw it away, and here's why: I don't intend to ever have another bypass surgery, so I won't be needing it. That's a big deal for me. In fact, that might be one of the biggest things I end up throwing out. We'll see.

How are you doing? What are we up to? Must be at

least five or six things already, without counting multiples. Write them down; add them up. Okay, let's lighten
up a bit. While we're still in the bathroom, let's take a look
at your makeup. Now, this will be fun.

When I worked at Avon and was visiting with members of the field organization, I met a wonderful, devoted
customer who was outraged that her favorite eye shadow
had been discontinued. "It was sort of a fluorescent sea-
foam-green color," she said. "I was wearing it thirty years
ago when I first met my husband and I've been wearing
it ever since. I'm not even sure he'll like me as much
without it." (Amazing where we get these ideas, isn't it.
But I've heard that comment more times that I can count
when it comes to changing makeup color.) Well, I had
the devil's own time convincing her to try something
new. "You can wash it off if you don't like it," I said.
"It's just makeup." She begrudgingly settled for a lovely
celadon green that, honestly, made her look at least ten
years younger. I kept in touch with her and she told me a
week later that her husband loved her new look. In fact,
she was so thrilled with his response that she changed
her lipstick and blush colors, too. The last time I spoke
to her she was going to experiment with a totally different hair color.

Green Tip: Beauty and the Box

It's time to get rid of all that makeup from your old look, but what to do with all the old containers? Cosmetics companies are starting to jump on the recycling wave, too. If you bring your old containers to M·A·C or Kiehl's, they offer free products in return. That way you clear out the old you and start off the new one without even spending more money! Sounds like a good deal to me! Check their Web sites for more information.

So what about you? Got some old makeup in that cupboard that looks tired? I do. I always had this thing about lip liners. It's probably because a long time ago, a makeup artist reprimanded me for not carefully outlining my lips before I applied lipstick. As is typical of me, I took his advice to an extreme and bought a whole bunch of lip liners in an assortment of different colors from hot pink to blood red—most of which looked really bad on me. (Abigail, my younger daughter, actually told me that one of them made me look "frightening." Probably the blood-red one.) Anyway, I still have them, just in case, I guess, they suddenly look really good. They're going out. Do you have a bunch of those little samples that cosmetics companies give you when you buy something? Do you ever use them? If you haven't by now, you're not going to. Throw them out.

Before we leave your makeup shelves and drawers, there's a question I'd like to ask you: What *do* you want to look like, anyway? Now's the time to reinvent yourself, to let go of some old notion of your look. It's funny, but ever since I was in college I've thought of myself as the dark type. My hair growing up was dark brown with reddish highlights—but when I saw a girl who sat in front of me in biology class my freshman year who had beautiful raven hair, I decided to imitate her. It turned out she used a Clairol wash-in color that was a dark, dark (very dark) brown. I used it, or something similar, for years. Twenty-five to be exact. And then a few years ago, a hairstylist in New York named David Evangelista asked me why I insisted on my hair being so incredibly dark. "Are you trying to look like Chita Rivera?" he asked. He never minces words. Now, Chita Rivera is a great-looking woman and a tremendous talent, but his point was that I'd created a look for myself that wasn't really in sync with who *I* was. "Let's get some highlights," he said. "Let's take some chances. Let go and live, Gail, what're you afraid of? We can always change it back."

Well, I went from just a few highlights applied by the extraordinary colorist at the John Barrett salon named Parvin Klein, to becoming nothing short of a blonde, to chestnut hair with red highlights, to . . . well, you get the picture. As I'm writing this, I'm wondering what Parvin and I will come up with in two weeks when my color appointment comes due. Who knows? Maybe I'll go back to Chita. A lot of good things happened in my life when my hair was that color. On the other hand, my mother was a platinum blonde, which I always admired—maybe it's time for me to take that leap. David is thrilled with my spirit of adventure. "It's all about change," he says. "With every single one of my clients, I really instill the notion that change is good and necessary to help one evolve and eventually become the person he or she is meant to be, this lifetime. So look in the mirror and see the person looking back because the change that you want is staring right at you."

By the way, I hate to remind you but all those lipsticks that are now lying in the wastebasket only count as one.

Here's the point: Get rid of any old notion of yourself or what your look is. As you throw out the old makeup and tubes of hair color, throw out your old idea of yourself. Write down that old idea in the column called MENTAL MAKEUP THROWAWAYS. You can always go back to some old look if the spirit moves you. Right now we're moving forward. Exactly how do you want to look? Exactly who do you want to be? You get to decide.

Rinse, Lather, Throw Out

We haven't even talked about what's inside your shower! I bet you have at least five different shampoos and conditioners, but I also bet there are probably only one or two that you use every time you wash your hair. Toss the ones you don't use, even if they're half full. You don't need them. And to get rid of the clutter, why not invest in a nice shower caddy with slots for all your necessities and hooks to hang washcloths and loofahs?

It's fun to reinvent yourself. The first time I did it was when I was ten years old and went away to camp in Vermont. Coming from Ohio seemed kind of pedestrian to me at the time, and I knew there would be girls at my camp from exotic places like São Paulo, Paris, Sydney, and even Hong Kong. So I decided to develop a new accent—something sort of bordering on Russian with a hint of French to soften it. Of course, I didn't speak either of those languages—nor did I have any real idea what they really sounded like—but that didn't matter. I arrived in camp with my "accent" intact and managed to intrigue a few girls who asked where I was from (I replied that it was a dark secret) before I forgot myself and asked for seconds on dessert in my regular voice. The interesting thing is, silly as it sounds, I taught myself a valuable lesson. **You can make yourself up anytime you want to. And if you do it with enough conviction and élan, the world will buy it. At least for as long as you do. Then everything's up for grabs.**

Steps for clearing the clutter in your bathroom:

1. Go for the old and expired stuff first—the old medicines, nearly dried-up cans of hair spray, toothpaste, used-up lipsticks, cosmetics samples that you're really never going to use—and dump it. Remember to put cans and the like in the proper containers. And don't throw prescription drugs down the toilet. There's recent evidence that certain drugs could end up in our drinking water and be dangerous. Check with your local pharmacy.

2. Now look more carefully at what remains. Are the medicines necessary and appropriate to how you feel or want to feel *now*? Are the cosmetics and toiletries representative of how you want to look *now*? If the answer is no, you know what to do.

3. Remember, you're making some fundamental decisions about yourself in this room. You're deciding how you're going to care for yourself, how you'll guard your well-being, going forward. Keep what serves that objective; let the rest go.

4. There are a lot of generic things in the bathroom—a dozen old bottles of nail enamel only count as one—so I doubt that you'll add an awful lot to your total numbers. Still, getting rid of this stuff sure will make you feel terrific.

Gail's Throw-Out Scorecard:

31 containers of prescription drugs for "old migraines" and other expired medicines

8 old ugly lipliners and 9 old ugly lipsticks from my old makeup and skin care samples

1 blower used to clear my lungs following my coronary bypass surgery, known as "Gail's heart caper"

Total: 4 things
Running Total: 7 things

Your Throw-Out Scorecard:

_____

_____

_____

_____

_____

Your Total:
Your Running Total:

Chapter 3

Your Kitchen

Well, I'm standing in the kitchen now. It looks okay on the surface except I'm wondering if I really do need to keep all those back issues of food magazines. Some of them go back over five years. They're taking up an awful lot of counter space. I think I was worried about not being able to find the recipes I want without the magazines. Everybody in our family cooks, and we're always looking for great new ideas. But now that I think about it, I can find all the recipes I want from all those magazines online. Okay, so here's what I'm deciding: I'll only keep the issues from the last three months. The rest can go. Boy, that's going to be at least sixty or seventy magazines. Too bad they only count as one.

A Recipe for Uncluttering

Cooking magazines are great, but they tend to accumulate fast. Luckily, most of the recipes are now archived online, where you can find them fast.

If you have some favorites, why not print them out and keep them in a folder—that creates a lot less clutter than seventy old magazines. Here are some of my favorite online recipe sites:

- www.gourmet.com
- www.cookinglight.com
- www.epicurious.com
- www.foodnetwork.com
- www.allrecipes.com

The cupboards don't look too bad—except for all the empty pickle, olive, mustard, and relish jars that my husband, Jim, collects. There are at least a dozen of them. He thinks he'll need them to store his own concoctions of condiments. He obviously hasn't discovered plastic, stackable containers, or ziplock bags. On the other hand, what I've learned the hard way is: *Don't throw out other people's stuff.* It can make them really mad. I'll never forget when my mother, with the very best intentions, went through our refrigerator and threw out all Jim's "old" jars of condiments. When he discovered his newly organized and pristine refrigerator, he went ballistic. It took several months before my mom even opened the refrigerator door without looking over her shoulder. And once, thinking it was a bag of trash, I threw out Abigail's collection of CDs. It was nothing short of a tragedy. So be careful. *Their* stuff is *theirs* to keep or throw away.

What about the pantry? We have a closet in our kitchen where we keep all our canned goods, our herbs and spices, all our baking ingredients, many bottles of different kinds of vinegars and oils, and multiple bottles and cans of various kinds of olive oil. We also keep all the boxes of pasta, nuts, crackers, and other kinds of dry foods in there. As I'm looking at it now, I can see probably five different little cans of cayenne pepper scattered around the spice area. "Why?" you might ask. It's because Jim forgets that he already has it and buys another one just in case. Well, I'm not going to throw them out, but I am going to at least gather them up into one place inside a ziplock bag. I'm also going to take a sniff of some of these spices that look a little old and tired. "Dried" is one thing; tasteless is another. Cooking (and eating) are too important to us to mess it up with colorless, tasteless ingredients. As a matter of fact, I think I'm going to take everything out of the closet, examine every last box, bottle, or can, clean them up, gather them together in some neat boxes or baskets from the Container Store, and replace them in a freshly painted, freshly organized closet. I feel good just thinking about doing it.

Green Tip: What's Under the Sink?

I bet I know what's under your sink—cleaning products, maybe a trash can, and probably lots and lots of bags from the supermarket. We all keep these bags because we want to reuse them some day, but let's face it, you probably never will and you keep collecting more and more. I say trash them, and just get a few nice canvas bags to take with you to the grocery store every time. It's better for the environment; plus, many stores will give you money off your order for using them. It pays to be green!

But what about "that drawer"? You know that drawer—full of everything that doesn't go anywhere else. Open it. If you can. Mine is so full it gets stuck. But after I yank it open, here's what I see:

- Old tubes of dried-up Krazy Glue.
- Dozens of old receipts from the grocery store.
- A whole lot of loose change, mainly pennies.
- Lots of paper clips, rubber bands, and those twist-it things.
- Hunting and fishing licenses for every member of the family that go back to 2000.
- Golf tees that have seen better days (and probably better golf).
- Lots and lots of AA batteries, most of which have expired.
- A tiny puppy collar for Willa (she weighs sixty-five pounds now).

- Three golf balls that have been badly chewed by guess who?
- A bunch of keys that haven't opened up anything in probably ten years. In fact, I have no idea what they're for.

Everything's going in the TRASH bag except Willa's collar, and that's going to hang over the corner of a picture of her as a puppy. She looked like a little yellow fur ball. How did she get so big so fast? Abigail says we should get another puppy just so we can still have a fat little fur ball around . . .

Take Charge of Your Batteries

When you ventured into "that drawer," you found lots of old batteries, right? You can throw them out; you just need to be careful. Place single-use batteries in plastic bags before you toss them. You can drop off your old rechargeable ones (including cell phone and laptop batteries) at Radio Shack. The store is partnered with the Rechargeable Battery Recycling Corporation (www.rbrc.org) to recycle them into new batteries or other products.

Actually, I haven't met anyone who doesn't have "that drawer" in their kitchen. People are always writing me about the crazy and interesting things they find in there. One guy found an old paper napkin where, many years earlier, he'd written an idea for a screenplay. He's decided it's a better idea now than it was then so he's developing it further and plans to pitch it to a film studio. Hey, you never know.

A woman named Liz wrote me about finding an old chocolate cake recipe from her mother—written on a three-by-five card decades earlier—when she cleaned out her pantry. She'd forgotten all about it. She sat there on the kitchen floor thinking about all the cakes her mom had made and all the occasions those cakes had celebrated. Her mom's gone now, and Liz was wishing like crazy that she'd told her how terrific those cakes were. I suggested she bake her mom's chocolate cake for her family and decorate it with the words THANKS MOM. She did, and she, her husband, and their kids drank a toast to Liz's mom's cakes that night at dinner. Nice, huh?

So what have you got in there? Anything worth keeping? Most of it goes, right? **Boy, it will feel awfully good to open that drawer from now on, won't it? It's like an unused corner of your mind that you can fill with good thoughts. Select carefully what you put in there. That drawer has gone from a total joke to a showpiece. Don't mess it up.**

By the way, until a couple of months ago it never

occurred to me that "Throw Out Fifty Things" could be a stand-up comedy routine. But then I met Marychris Melli. She brought in her list of throw-aways and presented each item to me along with the story behind it. I finally had to ask her to stop because I had a stomachache from laughing so hard. Her kitchen drawer had a lot of great throw-outs—especially involving her dog, Quixote. She threw out his antidepressant pills. "Let's face it, he's nuts," she said. She threw out his dog comb and said, "Like a comb would ever do the trick. I've got to accept that I've adopted a crazy white mutt who needs to be brushed for twenty minutes a day with a special tool that's sold only on an infomercial and this just isn't it." She threw out his nail clippers, too. "That's just wishful thinking," she said. "His nails are the least of his problems."

And then she told me what has become my favorite kitchen-drawer story. It revolves around the old folder Marychris found there—a folder that definitely had to go. Here's the story: Marychris was thirty-five years old and going through a really tough period in her life. She wasn't working, was attending graduate school, had amassed a lot of debt, had to sell her car, and wasn't paying much attention to anything except just getting through. One very rainy night after school she got in her old jalopy (she'd paid three hundred dollars for it so you can imagine the shape it was in) to head home. Suddenly she heard sirens. Three cop cars surrounded her and shouted at her to pull over. They told her to get out of her car and said there were two warrants out for her arrest—for unpaid parking tickets. Marychris had completely forgotten about the tickets and was trying to explain that to the cops as they put her up against her car and searched her.

"You have to picture this," she said. "My old jalopy and I are stopped on a main street in my little town in New Jersey, with cops surrounding me, drenched with rain, crying, up against my car with people I knew flying by in their cars. It was straight out of a movie." Then the cops discovered that her license had not only expired but had been suspended the day before. She was driving illegally.

"Okay, so this definitely wasn't the most organized time in my life," she said, "but wait till you hear this: I was handcuffed. Handcuffed! Can you believe it? Thrown into the back of a cop car and arrested!" It gets worse. They had to take her to the actual town where the crime had been committed, so on the town line they transferred her from one cop car to another in the next town—which meant she had to have new handcuffs put on by the new cop. She could hear over the car radio, "Transferring the prisoner . . ." *Prisoner?* she thought. *I'm a prisoner?* The new cops took her to the police station in the new town to book her.

"They took my mug shot," she said. "There I was, holding up numbers, crying and looking like Nick

Nolte." By this time it was eleven thirty at night and Marychris was told that if the fines ($163.50) weren't paid in cash, she'd be put in jail. She was allowed one call. She called her mom. But her mom didn't have enough cash and didn't believe in ATM cards (which is another story), so she had to go knock on a neighbor's door and ask for the exact amount. Evidently, police stations don't make change. When she got to the police station, well after midnight, Marychris had to restrain her mom from giving the cops a good piece of her mind—which probably would've landed both of them in jail for the night.

So what was in the folder in the kitchen drawer? Receipts. Receipts from paying the bail, receipts from the court fees, and a letter from the Bureau of Motor Vehicles stating that all the fines from the parking tickets had been paid in full. "It's all going out," she said. "I'm just not that person anymore. Then I had no money, a lot of debt, bad credit, and an old jalopy. Now I have a new car, my credit is good, and I finished grad school. I'm throwing out the memory of a time in my life when I just didn't have my act together. I do now. But it's a great story, isn't it?"

"One of the best," I told her. Quixote's still going strong, by the way, even without all his stuff.

You know, you could consider presenting your list of kitchen throw-outs to somebody in your family or to a friend. Go for the humor; crack them up; tell them about all the dumb stuff you allowed to collect in there. Maybe you'll motivate them to clear out their kitchen, too. Hey, what do you think stand-up comedy is created out of? Just silly day-to-day experiences that anyone can identify with—and what you're throwing out in your kitchen, or any other room for that matter, can make for great material. It's better used as material for comedy than as clutter in your life. Go for it!

Steps for clearing the clutter in your kitchen:

1. Ask yourself what this room represents to you. In our family the kitchen is all-important, because we're in love with food and cooking. So in addition to our needing things to be easily accessed, the atmosphere needs to be appealing. We have speakers for our cooking music, plenty of places for people who aren't cooking at the moment to sit and chat, and plenty of votive candles to help set the mood. It could be entirely different for you. But whatever it is, don't let the clutter sabotage the room's purpose.

2. Throw out any old, tired things, from banged-up pots to stale ingredients. We've decided we won't keep pots and pans that don't make whatever we're cooking look good. So when there are sales in catalogs or department stores, we take the opportunity to upgrade our stuff.

3. Ask members of your family or good friends what they'd like to add to or subtract from the kitchen. Our daughter Kate said she didn't like seeing barbecue equipment out in the open, so we found space for it in a closet. Abigail suggested we stack all our water bottles in a good-looking urn instead of leaving them in the plastic crate they come in. It looks great.

4. The kitchen—especially the counters—seems to be the catchall for just about everything. Don't let that happen. It's a great room for a great purpose. A lot of wonderful things can happen in a kitchen; don't let anything stand in the way—including "that drawer."

Gail's Throw-Out Scorecard:

65 food magazines

11 jars of old spices

7 jars of Jim's nearly empty pickle, mustard, and onion jars (I hope he doesn't get mad at me . . .)

Everything in "that drawer" except Willa's puppy collar

3 banged-up aluminum pans

Total: 5 things

Running Total: 12 things

Your Throw-Out Scorecard:

_____

_____

_____

_____

_____

Your Total:

Your Running Total:

Chapter 4 | # Your Living Room

We haven't approached our living or dining rooms yet, have we? Let's do it.

My living room is relatively tidy and well organized. ("Relative to what?" you might ask. "Your kitchen?") No, really, we spend so much time in our kitchen and our dining room/den that the living room is in pretty good shape. Don't you find that your living room is the least cluttered? I mean, still cluttered, but not as much? It probably depends on how old your kids are. When Kate and Abigail were little, the living room had a cardboard playhouse in it that took up a quarter of the room and a rocking horse named, appropriately, "Rocky" that took up another quarter. Plus, boxes of blocks and toys. I wouldn't have traded those cluttered days for anything. But now I have no excuse.

In our house, there is an entire wall of bookshelves separated by three windows that look out on the street. The shelves are filled with books from the last three and a half decades of reading. Some go back as far as college and graduate school. There's *From Agamemnon to Aristotle,* a thick compilation of Greek plays that I studied my freshman year at Sweet Briar College. I'll keep that as well as other anthologies; I might want to look something up at some point.

Oh, and speaking of plays, here's a paperback version of *Waiting for Godot* by Samuel Beckett. I can't throw that out. I played Vladimir, one of the two male leads in an all-girl cast in college. I played a ton of boys' parts at Sweet Briar. My low voice and lack of the typical female ingenue attributes—long hair, blue eyes, fair skin—sealed my fate as a guy. Actually, I had a ball. My favorite role was the devil in *Damn Yankees* my freshman year. I loved it. Along with my roommate who played Lola, I pretty much walked away with the show. Actually, I remember most of the lyrics from "Those Were the Good Old Days," my signature song. I think I'll sing it right now. "I see Bonaparte, a mean one, if ever I've seen one, and Nero fiddlin' through that lovely blaze; Antoinette, dainty queen, in her quaint guillotine, ah, ha, ha, haaa, those were the good old days . . ." Good thing no one but Willa is around.

How about you—is this where you keep your old books and stuff from school? Looking through them brings back a lot of memories, doesn't it? I remember Dr. Nelson, the head of the English Department at Sweet Briar, who taught Shakespeare. Because of him, I fell head over heels in love with the Bard of Avon. Or maybe it was with

Dr. Nelson. You won't be surprised to hear that I played Bottom in *A Midsummer Night's Dream,* will you?

So far, I don't see anything to throw out. Do you? I could be tempted by an old, outdated, unabridged dictionary that was given to Jim and me by a dear, departed friend as a wedding present. It must weigh at least twenty-five pounds. And it's badly chewed, not by Willa, but by Thai, our German shepherd. We bought Thai the day we got home from our honeymoon. What a great dog. Tough but great. He was actually my first "child." I felt so bad about leaving him at home that one day I brought him to work. Thai wouldn't allow anyone in my office. Boy, was that dumb. I mean, this was way before Take Your Child to Work Day. My boss told me never to do that again; this was an ad agency not an animal shelter, for God's sake.

Boy, I loved that dog. Unfortunately several years later, when I was pregnant with Kate and Jim was producing the eleven o'clock news at WCBS-TV in New York, Thai, who weighed 130 pounds, went after me and pinned me to the floor. I don't know why; something just came over him. I'd reached over him to pick up that twenty-five-pound dictionary to check a word I was writing for a management presentation and I guess something snapped in his mind. For several minutes, I lay still with Thai's mouth inches away from my throat and told him what a good boy he was and that Jim (his favorite person) was coming home right now. That got his attention, and he turned toward the door. I leapt up, ran out of the room, closed Thai inside, and waited for Jim to come. The following day we drove out to Long Island and gave Thai up for adoption to a man who ran a wonderful kennel there. I still remember the look of bewilderment and betrayal on Thai's face as we drove away. We both cried all the way back to New York.

A lot of these books have been chewed by Thai. I think they'll all stay.

I've just added quite a few things to my THINGS I'M KEEPING AND WHY column, haven't I? I'd better get crackin' on the throw-outs.

Well, in a lovely old hutch, stacked in the back, I see at least twenty-five or thirty record albums in their jackets. You know, the old $33\frac{1}{3}$ long-playing type. Boy, there's Frank Sinatra, Simon and Garfunkel, Edith Piaf, Marlene Dietrich, Mel Brooks and Carl Reiner comedy routines, a wonderful record by Herb Alpert and the Tijuana Brass with a drop-dead song by Herb called "You See This Guy?" ("This guy's in love with you . . .") What made that song so incredibly good was that Herb couldn't really sing. He played the trumpet and he played it brilliantly; he wasn't trained as a vocalist. But when he sings this song it absolutely grabs your heart because it's sung so honestly—not brilliantly but somehow, beautifully. I think I'll play it now. You know, these old LPs would be hard to replace. Wait, no they won't. I can get them as CDs or online.

The technology for getting the music we want in the form we want, at the price we want to pay (or no price at all), is changing and improving almost at the speed of well, sound. So I think I'll have to bite the bullet and throw out these old records. Or I can give them away or possibly sell them to a collector. Actually, I find this a tough letting-go. It would have been tempting to procrastinate and just keep them another year or so. But look, we can't just keep reopening drawers, closets, and hutches and seeing the same old useless stuff. It's suffocating and energy robbing and we're over that . . . (Remember, if you have to weigh for too long the pros and cons of throwing something out, it goes.)

Green Tip: When There's Nothing Good on TV

Are you upgrading your old television set for a new plasma flat screen? Instead of just sticking the old one on the curb, consider a new Sony program with drop-off locations around the country to help recycle them.

What I do see in this hutch is a lot of miscellaneous paperback books of no particular consequence. There are mediocre novels and, dare I say, how-to books that I either didn't read or—if I did read them—didn't follow. (You're not going to do that, are you?) And I can give at least fifteen or twenty of them to hospitals or community centers where they're always looking for books for the people they serve. I work out in a community center on the weekends, and they frequently have tables of old books there for the taking. They've just gotten a new (and ongoing) donor. (Wait till you read about Beth Comstock and her books in chapter 8. You'll love it. Also, see the resource guide at the end of this book for information on how to digitize and de-clutter your library as well as where to donate books.)

Let's Book It

It's hard to throw out books. Maybe someone gave you one as a gift. Maybe you bought a novel for a vacation and never got to it. You always think you will someday. But we're not talking about somedays here, we're talking about now. If it's a book you love, keep it. If it reminds you of an unhappy time or you're pretty sure you're never going to read it, then toss it or donate it to your local library. They may have book sales to raise funds. Another great way to get rid of books is through a program called Books for Soldiers (www.booksforsoldiers .com). You can put together books, DVDs, games, and other relief supplies into a box for shipment sent to troops abroad. Sometimes they make specific requests, but mostly they're just looking for anything to read.

What else? The small drawers of the end tables on either side of the sofa are crammed with an awful lot of odds and ends. Sort of reminds me of that kitchen drawer. There are quite a lot of photographs taken with Polaroid cameras—most of them not very good. Here's one of the back of somebody's head and another of a foot. Great shots taken who knows how many years ago by a crackerjack photographer named Jim. This is easy, there must be a couple of fistfuls of them. I find that, in general, photographs present a special problem. It's just so hard to throw them away. Especially photos of the children. (Oops, here's one of Abigail I wouldn't trade for anything. It shows her at a family dance at a beach club on Long Island at the age of three, having just knocked a little boy, I think his name was Matthew, to the floor; she seems to be climbing on him. I guess that was her own special way of inviting him to dance.)

Photo Finish

You've probably found tons of old photos tucked in drawers around your house just like I have. Toss the ones that didn't come out—you know you have many. As for the rest, if they're taking up too much room, why not scan them onto your computer or onto CDs? Then you can e-mail them to friends and family around the globe to relive your memories together (even if you're far apart).

I've made several videotapes (now DVDs) using shots of Kate and Abigail as they were growing up, sometimes interspersed with video, and always set to wonderful music. They were always embarrassed when I showed them at birthdays (I guess that's understandable, given that I included shots like the one of Abigail and Matthew), but they'll get a kick out of showing them to their own children one day. I did the same thing for my parents to celebrate special birthdays and anniversaries. I created a video for my father's eightieth birthday, with shots of him and my mom from their earliest days together, and set it to Louis Armstrong singing "It's a Wonderful World." I'm proud of those tapes; they really marked some pretty special moments. But they don't solve the problem of all the miscellaneous photos and what to do with them. I have a supremely organized friend who has each year, without fail, made new albums of photos of her children, carefully labeled and with running commentary underneath each shot. I was always sure I'd have done that if I weren't a crazed working mother—but actually, I don't think I would have. I mean, I'm just not that organized. Oops, wait a second. I'm organized, all right, I'm just not as organized as my mom. See? It takes practice to get rid of the old negative stuff in a permanent way. Well, at least I caught myself. And you've got to catch yourself, too, if as you go through this process you beat yourself up about how you should have done it sooner or better. We're here *now*. And we're doing it *now*. And it turns out that *now is exactly the right time*.

So all the miscellaneous photos go out. I've got the videos, after all. And all the really good pictures are in frames. It's okay to let them go. It's okay for you, too.

Steps for clearing the clutter in your living room:

1. This is the main room for entertaining, right? So you want people to feel really wonderful when they walk in. Walk into your living room as if you're a guest who's just arriving for a party. How does it make you feel? How would you like to feel? What will you change so that you can feel that way?

2. Consider moving everything around, including the furniture. This is one of the best ways I can think of to see any room with new eyes. Don't make a big deal out of it or try to make it perfect. Pretend you've just moved in and move things around randomly until you see an arrangement you like. Then start building your new room around it. Whatever doesn't fit easily into your new arrangement, whatever doesn't mean anything to you or serve a purpose, goes out.

3. Gather up things like glass objects, candleholders, pictures—anything that you think is charming—into inviting or even surprising arrangements. When the "things" seem to be taking over the room, remove them—one arrangement at a time. Put them in boxes for a garage or tag sale. Check chapter 7,

"Your Garage,"and the resource guide at the end of the book for more information.

4. Ask yourself what's the best memory you have of this room—was it a party, a family gathering, a meaningful moment with someone you love? Can you imagine reprising a moment like that now? Is there anything in the room that would get in the way? Remove it. Throw it away.

Gail's Throw-Out Scorecard:

> 33 paperback books
> 27 LP records
> Dozens of old photographs
>
> Total: 3 things
> Running Total: 14 things

Your Throw-Out Scorecard:

Your Total:
Your Running Total:

Chapter 5

Your Dining Room

The dining room might be my favorite room. As I've said, everyone in our family loves to cook, loves to eat, loves to talk about cooking and eating, loves to pore over old recipes and dream up new ones. Last night, the four of us cooked dinner together and honestly, it was spectacular. Jim made his now famous lobster pasta—a fragrant sauce made with artichoke hearts and garlic stewed in sweet vermouth, and served with black linguine. He only makes it on special occasions (the four of us having dinner together is not all that infrequent, but it sure is special) for two reasons: The ingredients are expensive, and it takes several hours to create. But the result is breathtakingly good. So good that you can hear any one of us sighing with delight as another forkful of linguine enters our mouths. And everyone made something. Kate made an hors d'oeuvre of grilled cauliflower dipped in hoisin sauce, Abigail made a wonderful salad of arugula and onion with lemon truffle vinaigrette, and both of them oversaw the delicate creation of the pasta sauce. But of course, the actual meal, and the eating of it, was way less important than the conversation and just the fact, the delight, of our being together—of loving one another and knowing that we do. Even now, writing about last night makes my heart, not just my stomach, feel full.

"What did *you* create, Gail?" you're probably wondering. And the answer is, the *ambience*. I might as well confess right now that I have a candle fetish. Actually, a dear friend of mine, Patricia Miller, made that pronouncement at a dinner party a couple of years ago when, thanks to my scattering scores of votive candles on every available surface, her husband Roger's jacket caught on fire. (You know that smell of wool burning?) Well, anyway, it wasn't anything serious, and Roger was an incredibly good sport about it, but you can see that candles—actually lighting in general—are extremely important to me.

I'm constantly replacing burned-down candles. Replacing them, but not throwing them out. I don't know why but I've got boxes of candles that are burned down two-thirds of the way. They're in the hutch that holds the dinner plates. I guess I've kept them in case there's another good old New York blackout. Well, they're getting thrown out. In order to create the serene, at times, even enchanting, dining environment that's the backdrop for the kind of intimate conversations we love to have, I can't have a bunch of crummy-looking burned-down old candles lying around, even if they're out of sight.

Green Tip: Waxy Buildup

Instead of throwing out all your old candle scraps, you can turn them into a fun recycling craft project. It's as simple as adding essential oil to the melted wax and letting it cool in a new container around a wick. You'll have a great new candle you can display in about an hour!

Also in that cupboard, I've got a lot of old cloth napkins, some of them pretty ratty looking, as well as some worn-out-looking place mats. No point in keeping them; we haven't used them in years. There are also some old dishes, one particularly ugly "corn dish" that's made to look like ears of corn laid end-to-end with their kernels etched into the china. Jim can't stand it. Do you have a dish or bowl like that? Just about everybody does. I think it was a wedding present, which makes it more than thirty years old. It and six other plates with a tiny flower design will be good for the tag sale. It's not that there's anything really wrong with the plates, it's just that I haven't ever used them, even when we've had large parties. That must mean something.

Seriously, when you run into something that someone, whom I'm sure had the very best of intentions, gave you that you've had for better than a decade but haven't used, throw it out, give it away, or sell it. It's obviously not your thing. And it's okay. It could be somebody else's. Remember Carrie and the heart bracelet? Enough said.

I'll tell you what I'm not throwing out: a stack of kerchiefs that have adorned the necks of all three of our golden retrievers, including Willa. In fact, whenever any one of them emerged from the groomers, she was not only washed and brushed, with teeth cleaned and whitened (they really do whiten her teeth while they're freshening her breath), but totally fragrant and festooned in a dog kerchief reflective of the current season. And all those kerchiefs—some with pumpkins on them, others with four-leaf clovers, some with holly, there are tons of cute patterns—lie carefully laundered, ironed, and stacked in a drawer right next to our good linen napkins. Not a good juxtaposition, right? Probably not, but, well, that's how we feel toward our dogs—pretty much the way we feel about most of our dinner guests—lovingly. So if you ever come over to our house for dinner, you won't mind the occasional dog kerchief next to your fork, will you?

Ditching Dishes

Food banks or soup kitchens in your area are always looking for donations. If you have extra mismatched dishes and silverware, do some research into the services in your area to find out if they're accepting these kinds of donations.

What about *your* dining room? Does it reflect your own particular attitude? Does it help create the kind of environment you love—one suggesting that great conversations, not just delicious dinners, take place here? Do you feel happy when you walk into it, or is it just another room? There's so much data out there about how important it is for families to have one meal, preferably dinner, together. On CNN this morning, Dr. Sanjay Gupta reported a study showing that families who dine together on a regular basis are actually less stressed and healthier. And their children grow up eating more fruits and vegetables and have a tendency to be thinner and fitter than those who don't. Interesting, huh? When Kate and Abigail were very young, we didn't know any of those statistics; we just knew that dinner was the one time when we could all decompress, share the good and not-so-good parts of the day, and talk not only about what was going on in our individual worlds, but what was happening in the world in general. I don't think it's an accident that both Kate and Abigail were told in school that they had an unusually firm grasp on current events—and I must say, they still do. I smile when I remember how, four or five years ago when a guy friend of Kate's was coming over for dinner, he politely asked if he could bring anything. "An opinion," Kate answered.

But seriously, what can you toss out of that dining room of yours that could get in the way of your creating the kind of fun and memories that will make you smile years later? Maybe it's old plates, napkins, or burned-down candles; maybe it's a rug that depresses you, or an overly bright light fixture. You'll know. And you'll throw it out. By the way, it won't surprise you to know that when Kate and Abigail have friends over, they absolutely surround them with votive candles—big ones, small ones, scented and unscented. They've even found a fabulous outlet store in Pennsylvania where you can get all kinds of candles for two-thirds off the regular price. They're my girls, all right.

Steps for clearing the clutter in your dining room:

1. What's the single most important feeling you'd like a family member or guest who dines in this room to walk away with? For me, words like *delighted, enchanted,* and *inspired* come to mind. Are there things in the room that would detract from that feeling? Out they go.

2. What's the best time you ever had in this room? What did it look like and feel like on that day? How can you re-create it? What should stay; what should go? (Check out the resource guide at the back of this book as well as chapter 7, "Your Garage," for information about throwing garage sales.)

3. Put all your everyday plates and dishes in your kitchen area and your special china in the dining

room. Don't just display it; use it. Who's more important than your family?

4. If you remove the old stuff that depresses or displeases you, you'll have space to add some things that delight you. How about a mirror that reflects the wonderful faces of everyone who dines there (as well as the light from all your fabulous candles)? Or what about adding speakers so that you can play some wonderful background music? Or a giant vase filled with branches placed on the floor with an uplight behind it for dramatic effect? Am I getting carried away?

Gail's Throw-Out Scorecard:

39 old burned-down candles
15 old napkins
16 old place mats
1 ugly corn dish
6 pretty but not-my-type plates

Total: 5 things
Running Total: 19 things

Your Throw-Out Scorecard:

_____

_____

_____

Your Total:
Your Running Total:

Chapter 6 | # Your Attic

I'd like to talk about the attic for a minute. Actually, just talking about it makes me feel bad. Even walking past the door to the attic makes me queasy. Here's why: I haven't sorted out anything up there in years. I know it sounds terrible, but it's true. (See, this goes back to my mom's telling me I wasn't organized, and to that time she threatened to turn all my drawers upside down on the floor of my bedroom. I started to believe that organizing things successfully was obviously really hard and clearly something I'd never be good at.)

But I'm not the only one. Whenever anyone in our family doesn't know what to do with something, or doesn't want to decide what to do with it, they put it up in the attic. So in addition to the typical mattresses and box springs, the lamps, chairs, and headboards, and the boxes of old photographs and mementos, there is the furniture Kate and Abigail used in college, there are old rolled-up rugs, outdated appliances, dollhouses, children's games, a blackboard, a toy piano, a guitar, an African drum, many, many rolls of wallpaper (some of it chewed up, but not by Willa), mirrors, chandeliers (some of them quite nice), and my wedding dress. Then there's a lot of miscellaneous stuff in boxes and bags that I haven't opened in years and can only imagine what I'll find when I do. But I'll get Abigail to help me. (Maybe we'll bring up a CD player and a bottle of wine.) Yup, there's definitely a garage or tag sale in my future. My near future.

On the surface, it might look pretty easy to decide what to keep and what to throw out, sell, or give away. I mean, obviously, I'm keeping the wedding dress. And it would be tempting to keep all the stuff that's in good shape or that Kate or Abigail might be interested in sometime in the future. But the operative word here is *might*. The last thing you want is to keep a lot of irrelevant stuff that they're going to feel guilty about tossing someday. So be selective about what you keep. I know Kate's and Abigail's tastes well enough that I can make pretty good decisions if I really think about it.

Color-Code Those Throw-Outs

In the *Sex and the City* movie, Carrie's packing up her whole apartment with the help of her best girlfriends before her wedding day. Charlotte comes up with a great system using different-colored Post-its. Everything is separated into keep, giveaway, and trash. You'll see later in this chapter that you can also use this system as you go through your attic.

There's absolutely no reason to keep the old college furniture, especially when someone else could put it to good use. With tuitions going up along with so many of our living expenses, buying new furniture for a college student just won't be in the cards for a lot of people. So I'm not going to sell it, I'm going to give it away. If you've got stuff like that, check out the resource guide at the end of the book for the best way to give it away.

But the appliances will go in the box for the tag sale, as will the mirrors, lamps, chandeliers, and rugs, except for the one my grandfather bought more than ninety years ago. It's a real beauty: It's Oriental, woven with deep reds and blues in a lovely design, and although it doesn't fit into any of my current color schemes, it has great sentimental value. When Kate and Abigail were babies, they played on that rug, just as my brother and I did. We have the pictures to prove it. The unchewed wallpaper, which is actually very pretty, will go on the wall of a bathroom or maybe inside a closet. (Papering the inside of a closet, especially one you've just cleaned out, can give you a real lift.) And I'll give the children's games, toy piano, and blackboard to our church. (Again, check the resource guide for great ideas on where to donate good stuff.) But the African drum stays. I mean, you just never know when the urge to start drumming might hit you.

Green Tip: Freon to Be You and Me

I bet there is an old air conditioner or two up in your attic. If it's still in working order, but you're never going to use it again, take it to Goodwill. If it's busted, call your sanitation department. Usually they will collect air conditioners and other Freon-containing appliances like watercoolers and dehumidifiers.

And of course, Kate's miniature violin stays. When Kate was about four years old, I heard that playing an instrument, particularly a violin, was immensely helpful in developing a young child's cognitive ability. So we bought a small-size violin and enrolled her in Suzuki violin classes. The Suzuki Method, as it is called, was invented in the mid-twentieth century by Shin'ichi Suzuki, a Japanese violinist who wanted to bring beauty into the lives of children in his country after the devastation of World War II. "I want to make good citizens." Suzuki wrote, "If a child hears fine music from the day of his birth and learns to play it himself, he develops sensitivity, discipline and endurance. He gets a beautiful heart." He pioneered the idea that any preschool-aged child could begin to play the violin if the learning steps were small enough and if the instrument was scaled down to fit his or her body.

Kate thrived in her one-on-one lessons with Phil Hough. Suzuki would have heartily approved of Mr. Hough. He was a very kind, soft-spoken, patient, and gentle man with a wonderful reputation for teaching young children. Kate took quite naturally to playing the violin and even practiced more or less when she was supposed to. Her best piece was called "Lightly Row"—she could play it all the way through in less than a minute. It was, as it turned out, the speed and not the music that appealed to her. Listening to her practice at full throttle after a hard day's work required two Extra-Strength Tylenol.

But the lessons went well until one day I made the mistake of correcting something she said to Mr. Hough and she replied, "No, pit head, that's not what I meant!" Although I stifled a laugh (a sense of humor, even bordering on sarcastic, was highly prized in our house and was not lost on Kate), the gentle Mr. Hough was clearly appalled that my daughter had called me a "pit head." "Well, I think it's time to bring this lesson to a close, don't you?" Mr. Hough said. I readily agreed. And Kate, who'd apologized for her rudeness without being asked, said as we walked home that she'd like to move on to the piano because there was absolutely no way she could play "Lightly Row" any faster than she already had. I said okay, and the little violin has stayed in its case ever since. Kate developed a "beautiful heart" anyway.

I wonder how Mr. Hough is. I think I'll give him a call.

All rooms are filled with memories, but it seems attics have way more than their fair share. My wonderful former assistant and dear friend Jane Blecher found that out recently. She came up with a system for tackling what might be the most intimidating room in the house—and lived to talk about it.

Jane's mom died nearly a year ago at the age of ninety-three, and Jane and her sister have been in the throes of sorting out her things for months. None of it has been easy, but the attic was the biggest challenge. "When I first went into my mom's attic, I couldn't get past the doorway," Jane says. "I had to lean up against the wall and catch my breath. *What right do I have to go in here? Who am I to make these decisions? How can I throw my mother away?*" Jane went straight downstairs and called her best friend. "My darling friend told me something that to this day gives me the strength to keep going through all this whole sorting-out process. 'The memories are in your heart,' she said, 'not in the stuff.'"

Jane recommends setting up three big black trash bags. "Grab a Post-it and pen and label one bag TRASH, another KEEP, and the third SELL/DONATE, she says. "The stuff you find that you love and absolutely must have goes in the KEEP bag. But the stuff you put in the TRASH bag is done. You don't go back to it; the stuff in there is over." (By the way, it's worth noting that the things you put in the SELL/DONATE, bag are over, too—over for you, though possibly just beginning for someone else.)

Jane cautions us that the TRASH bag is going to be filled with "well, trash," as she puts it, and that you'll be digging out stuff with dust bunnies attached to it and grime that you don't want to touch any more than you have to. "Wear crummy clothes, something to cover your hair, and garden gloves to protect your hands.

"You get resentful," Jane continues. "You ask, *Why wasn't all this junk thrown out years ago? Why did my mom have to leave it for me?*" (You and I have to be really careful that we don't do the same thing . . .) "Be prepared to get really ticked off," she advises.

The KEEP bag should have a tissue box very close by. It's not just that you're going to be sneezing; there could be tears, too. You'll find things that you haven't seen in years. Maybe decades. Good things, bad things . . ." Jane sort of trails off here, and then she tells me the story of the fishing hat. "There was this really stupid fishing hat," she says. "It was canvas with *grommets,* for heaven's sake, that my mom and dad made me wear when we'd go on vacation to some lake. I'd have to put on the itchy orange life jacket—I was seven years old at this point—and get in the rowboat. Mom would put the hat on me and Dad would break out the fishing equipment. He was the worst fisherman ever. He'd row out to some spot that looked good, ship the oars, and then the boat would start rocking and I would turn green. I was the kind of kid who could throw up at, well, the drop of a hat. But my dad felt that if you threw up overboard, you'd scare away the fish. And that's where the little grommet-covered hat came in. I'd start getting all whiny and my mother would look at me sharply and whip that hat off and I'd throw up in it. Afterward, it would get thrown out and a new one would be acquired for the next adventure."

So as Jane was rummaging around in the attic the other day, she found this hat. Her dad had been gone for a long time, and she was wondering why in the world that hat was there. "I guess my mom just kept it as a memory," she says. "I pick up the hat and just look at it. One or two of the grommets are missing. It's a bit sweat-stained, but still smells faintly of my dad's wonderful cologne. He never went anywhere without his cologne. I hold out this hat to my sister and say, 'Look! Daddy's hat!' And she says, 'Hah! Guess that was the one that got away clean.' And I burst into tears. See? I told you the box of tissues was important." By the way, Jane's keeping the hat. You just never know when you're going to feel queasy.

Yup, attics can be bittersweet places. And knowing what to keep and what to let go of can seem like a daunting task. That's why we spend years talking about how we have to go up there and throw stuff out, but somehow never get around to it. My excuses go something like this: "It's too hot up there now. I'll wait till the fall." Or "The light's not working up there, it's too dark; I'll wait till the spring." I've got a million of 'em. But here's a little "Attic Questionnaire" I've prepared for myself—it's sort of a mini version of the Rules of Disengagement that applies to this most difficult of rooms. It's ridiculously simple, but it works:

- Do I really love it?
- Do I need it now?
- Can I imagine myself or anyone in my family ever loving or needing it in the foreseeable future?

If you can't answer yes to any one of these questions, throw it out. Because for you, it's over.

Oh, and the next time you go up there to stash something new—ask these exact same questions. And if you can't manage a yes, *stop*. Whatever you're holding in your hand gets tossed, with no looking back. It goes into the TRASH or the SELL/DONATE bag. Not in the attic.

One last thought: Be sure that what you do keep holds a good memory for you. Anything that reminds you of a difficult or negative experience or a time when you felt bad about yourself has to go; I don't care how valuable it is or what your mother would say. *We really are what we think about.* **And what we surround ourselves with influences a lot of our thinking—even if it's stashed way up in the attic. If it's still there, it still affects us. So don't make it hard, my friend, just let it go.**

Steps for clearing the clutter in your attic:

1. Attics are filled with both wonderful and not-so-good memories. Keep the things you love even if you'll never use them again. Absolutely everything else is up for grabs.

2. Remember, there are no *shoulds* to this process—no shoulds from you, none from your mother, none from anybody else. There's only what makes you feel good.

3. If you have to think too long about what to do with any item you come across, throw it out. And don't look back or second-guess yourself. Once it goes into the bag marked TRASH, or SELL/DONATE, it's done, as Jane says. You've got great instincts. Follow them.

4. Check out "Sally Carr's 'Good Stuff' Tag Sale" in chapter 7 so you can not only let go of this stuff, but have fun in the process. And above all remember: *The memories are in your heart, not in the stuff.*

Gail's Throw-Out Scorecard:

3 old chandeliers

2 old mirrors

4 folding chairs

2 sets of twin-size headboards

2 old rugs

1 toaster oven
8 boxes of children's games
1 blackboard
1 toy piano
1 guitar
3 rolls of chewed-up wallpaper

Total: 11 things
Running Total: 30 things

Your Throw-Out Scorecard:

_____

_____

_____

_____

_____

_____

Your Total:
Your Running Total:

Chapter 7 | # Your Garage

I think we're warmed up sufficiently to wander into the garage now. Although it reminds me a lot of the attic, when you think about it. It's just so darned easy to stow stuff away in there without making any decisions about whether to keep it or throw it out. The problem is, when you open the garage door, it really looks like the pits to anyone who's driving by. *What kind of people will they think we are, I ask myself, to have such a messy garage?*

Well, there's more of Kate's and Abigail's college furniture in here that I'd forgotten about. And some boxes from my parents' house that I didn't put into storage because I was going to go through them sooner rather than later. That was seven years ago. Now, that makes me feel bad.

Bicycles for the World . . . Not Your Garage!

When your kids get older, they need bigger bikes, but the smaller bikes tend to linger. There's a group in Washington called Bicycles for the World that collects bikes and sends them to people in developing nations who could become more productive with better transportation. They've sent thousands of bikes to places like Barbados, Costa Rica, the Gambia, Guatemala, Honduras, Namibia, and Panama. Do a little searching—there might be a group like this in your area, too.

I think that in one of the boxes, there are several pen-and-ink paintings done by my brother, Jay, which my parents always had hanging in their living room. Luckily, they're all beautifully wrapped, sealed, and boxed. My parents have been gone for several years. We lost Jay my senior year in college. He became a navy fighter pilot after graduating from Annapolis and was flight commander on the USS *Forrestal*. His plane crashed in the Mediterranean while he was executing a mock bomb run. Not to have opened those boxes is, I know, my way of avoiding the pain of all those memories, which like all first-degree wounds never quite heal. But I think it's time to carefully unpack those pictures and hang them up in our house. Or one or two of them might look wonderful in either Kate's or Abigail's apartments—or even in my office. Yes, it really is time to open those boxes. I'll dress the wounds as I go. But I'll also rekindle some really wonderful memories. Boy, we had terrific times together. We loved one another a lot. And we knew it. When the four of us were together, my mom always told us to "wrap our arms around the moment" . . . so that we really got it about how lucky we were. So that, no matter what, we could remember. I remember.

Recently, I rediscovered Thornton Wilder's novel *The Bridge of San Luis Rey*. The last paragraph means a lot to me. If you're missing someone you loved a lot, it might help you, too.

> We ourselves shall be loved and then forgotten. But the love will have been enough; all those impulses of love return to the love that made them. Even memory is not necessary for love. There is a land of the living and a land of the dead and the bridge is love, the only survival, the only meaning.

So as I'm filling up the boxes to be thrown out, with all the rusted tools, the old bags of no-longer-enriching topsoil, and even the old hammock that finally gave out when Kate, Abigail, and Willa piled into it, I'll be opening up other boxes and wrapping my arms around the love and memories that emerge.

How are you doing? Has something you've come across enabled you to rediscover or rekindle an old memory or an old love? Remember, once again, the Rules of Disengagement. If it makes you feel heavy or inadequate, it goes. If it stands for or reminds you of something good or important—something worth wrapping *your* arms around—it stays.

But look, you can't possibly want to keep that pair of training wheels for your daughter's two-wheeler, can you? I mean, she's eighteen now. And what about all those cans of paint, turpentine, and hopelessly dried-up brushes? (We should have soaked them in turpentine right after we used them, right?) A word about throwing out old paint: If you call your town hall, you can find out which day old cans of paint will be picked up at your local dump. They usually do it once a month. And if you live in the city, here's a trick the guy at my local paint store taught me to safely throw out old paint: Fill the old can with dirt and then sprinkle powdered concrete on top. Within an hour, the paint will have turned into a solid block of cement. Then you can simply throw it into the garbage.

Green Tip: Throwing Out Hazardous Waste

I'm sure you found all sorts of things in your garage—old paint, motor oil, antifreeze. Again, we don't want to throw these things out because we know they're hazardous to the environment. Many towns have a hazardous waste day when you can bring all of your items to one central location to professionals who know how to dispose of them. If you can't wait that long, check out www .earth911.org. It's a great Web site for finding local information on recycling all sorts of things.

And there can't be a reason to keep all these old garden pots. At least not the plastic ones. I'm going to keep a few of the clay pots and get rid of the rest. (Remember, they only count as one . . .)

There's actually a ton of stuff in here that needs to go. The question is, as with different things from many rooms in the house (like the attic): Where should it go? Well, it can go into a garbage can or into a Dumpster. My friend Richard Pine has one pulled up to his house right now and says it's one of the best things that ever happened to him. He's redoing a bathroom, and the Dumpster was brought in to get rid of all the old bathroom fixtures. But Richard likes it so much that he's keeping it around for a while and using it as a receptacle for just about everything he can think of that he doesn't need anymore. Actually, I hear fabulous things about Dumpsters. "Getting a Dumpster was one of the best things I've ever done for my family," one effusive woman e-mailed me recently. "When my youngest child went off to college, we brought in a Dumpster for ten days and absolutely everything went into it—from old school notebooks to broken-down 'Barbie Dream Pools.'" So that's one possibility. But there's another.

My friend Sally Carr, who lives in a small town in Connecticut, holds a garage sale every year. She invites everyone she knows to bring the stuff they want to get rid of to her house for the sale. And believe me, it's quite an event. "I've been doing tag sales and garage sales for forty years," Sally says, "and they just keep getting better and better." (For Sally's tips for giving the all-time best garage sale, see the end of this chapter.)

By "better and better," Sally not only means that more and more people participate and that it's become nothing less than the social event of the season, but also that the stories that go with the sales become funnier or more inspiring every year. And there's always a story: A woman who had lost her mother thirty years earlier was finally able to go through her clothes and accessories, and she brought them to Sally's garage sale. You can imagine what an emotional day that must have been for her. Her mother's gorgeous silk scarves were on sale for five dollars each and went like hot cakes. At first the woman was upset; it had taken her so long to even consider letting go of her mom's things, and here they were being snatched up by perfect strangers. But a few weeks later, she saw Sally wearing one of the scarves and she could see how much

Sally treasured it. "I know now that I did the right thing," she said.

And speaking of doing the right thing—Sally's garage sales aren't just for fun. "I consider my garage sales—and everyone else's—to be recycling at its best and highest use," Sally says. "Other than my pots and pans, absolutely *everything in my house is recycled.* You'll find eighteenth-century antiques along with items from our local cancer benefit rummage sale." At a recent luncheon in her dining room, a guest noticed a handsome oil portrait hanging on the wall.

"Is that your ancestor?" she asked. "No, it isn't," Sally replied. "I bought it at an auction." "Well," the woman said, "don't you think it's a bit pretentious to hang a portrait of someone you don't even know on your wall?" "Not at all," Sally responded. "As with all the things in my house, I'm just the caretaker. And this is a treasure I'm going to enjoy and care for—because someone else couldn't."

But Sally's commitment to recycling goes even further. "I'm teaching my grandchildren how important—and enjoyable—it is to use things for a while and then pass them on. When there's a tag sale, I give each of them a dollar, sometimes two, and encourage them to buy whatever toys they want. They have a wonderful time and find all kinds of interesting things," she says. "But what they're really learning is that if they can prevent just one piece of plastic from going into the landfill—by using other children's outgrown toys and then passing them on when they're finished with them—they'll be doing their share in going green."

Sally's motto is, "If you no longer need it, pass it on."

One more thing about Sally's garage sales: Every year she has a contest for the ugliest item. "Everyone votes," she says, "and the competition is fierce." But here's the funny part: No matter how unattractive, how badly designed, how downright ugly the item is, or how convinced you are that no one in their right mind would ever buy it, it's always the first thing to go. Always.

Sally Carr's "Good Stuff" Tag Sale:

THE TEN TIPS

1. **Set a date for your sale as well as a rain date.** Sally recommends the spring or fall. Check what else is going on in your neck of the woods. "You don't want to compete with a church bazaar," Sally says, "because that's not nice, but on the other hand, if there are several other tag sales going on, you can piggyback off each other."

2. **Choose a home, yours or someone else's, that has room for parking,** setting up tables, and browsing. "Our property has an old stone wall, which is the perfect place for people to display some of their wares," Sally says.

3. **Advertise a week or two in advance** in local newspapers, bulletin boards, and supermarkets, and distribute flyers in your area. Relegate your marketing to a twenty-mile radius of the actual event. "Gas is too expensive to expect people to drive farther than that," Sally advises. She also says, "Be sure to find out about items or categories such as linens, Wedgwood china, ironstone, one-drawer antique stands, or cherry queen-size beds so you can include those items in your ads."

4. **The day of the sale, post attractive, clear signs** in the neighborhood and near the main roads. "Always remember to remove all signs and ads immediately following the sale," Sally urges. "You don't want to be remembered for littering."

5. **"Name your sale,"** Sally advises. "Make it sound like fun. 'The Good Stuff Tag Sale' sounds like it won't be junk and you might just have a good time. And both are true."

6. **Charge each seller or participant a minimal fee** (usually about fifteen to twenty dollars) to help cover the costs of ads and refreshments. Sally and her husband, Larry, serve coffee and doughnuts to the participants during setup time, and Larry serves a wonderful lunch of Cajun hot dogs, hamburgers, macaroni and cheese, beer,

wine, and soft drinks later in the day. Their tag sales run from 9 a.m. to 4 p.m., with setup time scheduled from 7 to 9 a.m. They usually have ten to twelve participants (many of whom contribute something delicious for lunch) and 100 to 150 people attending. It's quite a party.

7. **Encourage each participant to clean, fix, wash, replace batteries, iron, polish, or do whatever it takes to make items more desirable.** "I can't stress this enough," Sally says. "Things that look good and are in good working order sell; things that aren't, don't. It's that simple."

8. **Encourage participants to market their wares by greeting potential customers,** engaging them in conversation, answering any questions, and demonstrating their wares. Many participants actually model the clothes they're selling—"which can be highly entertaining," Sally says.

9. **Remind participants to price their items carefully.** "This is a tag sale, not an upscale antiques shop or fancy boutique," Sally says. "Folks shop at tag sales to get a bargain, not to pay retail." Sally advises us to watch *Bargain Hunt* and *Cash in the Attic* on BBC America to get a sense of how to price household goods. "*The Antiques Road Show* has made some folks think almost anything old

is worth a lot of money and that's just not always the case," Sally says. But she also notes that people come raring to bargain, and your pricing should take that into consideration as well. "It's amazing to see how many participants buy from each other while also disposing of their own items. This is truly recycling at its best."

10. **Have fun; tell stories.** Many of the people who come to Sally's "Good Stuff" Tag Sale come year after year. It's easy to see why. In addition to awarding a prize for the most undesirable and ugliest item in the show, Larry and his friends always model truly outrageous outfits with equally outrageous price tags hanging from them. "You should see a seller give some unsuspecting buyer ninety-nine reasons why they need to purchase a particular item that has absolutely no value whatsoever," Sally says. "It's hilarious." Laughter and stories abound. And of course, as it turns out, the stories are equally important. "It can be kind of emotional when someone sells items that once belonged to their parents or someone else they've loved and lost," Sally concludes. "Sometimes they like to tell stories about the person they're missing and why this particular item was so special. It's important to listen. It helps in the letting-go."

Okay, by my account, *I'm past thirty things already,* even when I follow the rule that multiples of the same type or genre only count as one. You must be doing at least as well. So it's worth stating right now that there's nothing to keep you from going to seventy-five or a hundred or even beyond.

Now would be a good time to bring your list up to date and acknowledge yourself for how far you've come. There's nothing like positive reinforcement to give you the energy to persevere—and there are still miles to go. Remember, our aim is to clear the decks of the irrelevant past so that we can begin to build a future that's worthy not only of who we are now, but also of who we're becoming. As an old friend of mine used to say, "You can put hot fudge sauce over cat food but it's still cat food." Throw it out.

Steps for clearing the clutter in your garage:

1. Open up the garage door. How do you feel when somebody drives by and sees all the stuff in it? Who cares what they think anyway, right? But still. The garage seems to be a sort of way station for things we don't really want around but haven't decided to get rid of. Now's the time to get rid of them.

2. Except once again, you should keep the things that mean something to you, like a brother's pictures. And those things shouldn't be in the garage, any-

way. Put them where they belong, put them to use, or, as Sally says, pass them on.

3. Consider getting large containers with labels from the Container Store to hold the odds and ends of things you're actually using. Stack them in ways that are easily accessible but also attractive. When the entire area is all cleaned up and organized, think about painting the inside. Seriously, I know a guy who painted the inside of his garage geranium red after he cleaned it all out. It looks absolutely terrific. He loves looking at it.

4. Have a garage sale and invite everyone you know, including their kids, to come and bring not only stuff to sell, but stuff to eat and drink as well. Make it a party. Celebrate the passing on of good things (even if some of them are a little bit ugly).

Gail's Throw-Out Scorecard:

4 broken wicker baskets
14 old clay and plastic pots
8 cans of old paint and paint thinners
1 bag of plant fertilizer
1 wicker chest

Total: 5 things
Running Total: 35 things

Your Throw-Out Scorecard:

_____

_____

_____

_____

_____

Your Total:

Your Running Total:

Don't forget to log on to www.throwoutfiftythings
.com to keep track of your throw-outs and to share
your story with others. You can send us pictures
and videos of what you're tossing. Think of all the
people you'll inspire!

PART TWO

Your Office: Paring Down the Professional Clutter

| # Clarifying Your Brand

Well, much as I'd like to put it off, it's time to move into the office. Now, you might not have an office in the traditional sense: Fewer and fewer people do. Maybe you have a small office in your home or an area where you take care of business. It doesn't matter; the process of throwing out is still pretty much the same. Whether you're a budding entrepreneur, a corner-office titan, or you simply "occupy the ether," as one friend puts it, you've got to let go of what no longer serves you.

Steve Jobs is one of my all-time favorite entrepreneurs. He knows when to hold on and when to let go.

Several years ago, he gave the commencement address to the graduating class at Stanford and said a lot of wonderful, unforgettable things. I've given out at least a thousand copies of his speech. He talked about passion and faith and even death. "Death is very likely the single best invention of Life," he said. "It is Life's change agent. It clears out the old to make way for the new." That's exactly what you and I are doing right now, aren't we? "Your time is limited," he said, "so don't waste it living someone else's life. Don't be trapped by dogma—which is living with the results of other people's thinking. Don't let the noise of other's opinions drown out your own inner voice. And most important, have the courage to follow your heart and intuition. They somehow already know what you truly want to become. Everything else is secondary."

And then he told this wonderful story. "When I was young," he said, "there was this amazing publication called *The Whole Earth Catalog*." It was his bible, he said, published in the 1960s by a fellow named Stewart Brand, who created it with typewriters, scissors, and Polaroid cameras. He described it as a sort of "Google in paperback form . . . idealistic and overflowing with neat tools and great notions." He described how Stewart and his team had put out several issues of *Whole Earth*. And then when it sadly had run its course, it was time to let go—so they put out their final issue. On the back cover, Jobs said, was a photograph of a country road, sort of in the middle of nowhere: "The kind you might have hitched on as a kid." Beneath it were the words, "Stay Hungry. Stay Foolish." It was Brand's and his team's farewell message. "And I have always wished that for myself," Jobs concluded. "And now, as you graduate and begin anew, I wish it for you. Stay hungry. Stay foolish." And, my friend, I wish it for you and me as well.

> You can read Steve Jobs's commencement speech in its entirety here: http://news-service.stanford.edu/news/2005/june15/jobs-061505.html

I wish it weren't so hard to be brave enough to be foolish or to be secure enough to reach for something you might never be able to grasp. Still, I know that the real joy is not in the accomplishment, but in the struggle. And a good part of the struggle is in the continual letting-go of the past. That's the only way to change; to evolve; to become what you were meant to be. My father always said, "Stay light on your feet and ready to dance. The world is spinning too fast for you to be caught flat-footed. Fall in love with change."

Here's the bottom line: You can't be agile and ready to dance if you're locked in that block of marble with all the old presentation decks, rejected proposals, irrelevant data, and never-read books by the latest, greatest business gurus. Get out your hammer and chisel.

So while we're in the office, what have *you* got to throw out? Be brutal. Conservatively, I'm looking at about seventy-five or a hundred things right here, including all the books and documents. Unfortunately, they're all of one genre, so they're only going to count as one thing. But I think that's fair, don't you? Otherwise we'd both be done. And heaven knows, we're not. Not by a long shot.

How Long to Keep What

Your company may have a policy about what can be thrown out, what must be stored, and what must be shredded. Be sure you follow the rules. The main thing is to eliminate needless or negative stuff from your immediate surroundings. In your home office, you can use these general rules:

- Bank statements: Keep only what has relevance for tax purposes.
- Bills: Keep for one year, but make sure canceled checks have been returned.
- Credit card records: Keep any statements related to taxes for seven years; shred receipts after you see that they match up to your statements.
- Paycheck stubs: Keep for one year. You can shred when you receive your W-2 form and everything matches up.
- Retirement plan statements: Keep the yearly summaries until you retire, but shred the others if everything matches up.
- Tax returns and records: Keep for seven years.

And there are also companies like SiftSort (www.siftsort.com), where you can now have secure, portable access to important items such as tax

returns, financial statements, passports, medical
records, and insurance cards using a browser,
mobile device, e-mail, fax, or toll-free hotline.

If I sound like I kind of dreaded this particular
throwing-out assignment, it's because the mere thought
of going through my office comes close to overwhelming
me. As an entrepreneur, I've tried all sorts of different
approaches to my business during the last ten years. Some
have worked, some haven't, and each approach has its own
load of stuff that goes with it: from documents and pitches
to corporations, to ideas for books and workbooks and CDs,
to designs and copy for myriad Web sites, to what seems
like hundreds of presentation decks, thousands of pages
of notes about men and women whom I've coached, and
shelves filled with other people's books and manuscripts.

Whether you're an entrepreneur or not, you must
have similar files and folders crammed into cabinets and
drawers. The question is: How much of this stuff actually
has anything to do with who you are now, or what you're
becoming?

**To know what to throw out in our offices, we have
to know what our brand is. In other words, what's our
value proposition, as they say in advertising, or our
brand essence?** What's our promise? No matter who you
are, no matter what you do, you've got a brand. If you

don't create it, someone else will. And they might not make up something that fits with your best view of yourself. But you can.

It's absolutely vital to our success to *decide* (there's that word again) who we are at the core and what distinguishes us—or could distinguish us—from the herd. That means we have to *let go* of what doesn't serve our brand. When you look at it that way, it makes it much easier to throw out the stuff—not only in the closet but in the office, too—that no longer fits. For me, that's going to be all the documents and proposals where I was trying to fit myself (a round peg) into a square hole . . . all the times I pitched myself to corporations as an expert in organizational structure or crisis intervention. I'm just so not either of those two things. But the good news is that I know terrific people who are. And when I spot a need for one of those two skills—or any other skills that don't represent my brand— from one of my corporate clients, I can wholeheartedly recommend one of my colleagues.

What I *am* is much simpler than that: I'm a motivator. I help people discover how good they already are and show them how to bring their very best selves into the next great segment of their lives. Pure and simple. And everything I do—every speech I give, every column I write, every workshop I conduct, and every one-on-one coaching session I have with someone—has to make good on that promise. So anything that doesn't fit with that definition of my business goes. Conservatively, I'm looking at throwing out at least thirty major documents and proposals. For you it might be old files, presentation decks, or reports. I bet you've got a ton. See how easy it is to get to fifty? I should have called this book *Throw Out One Hundred and Fifty Things*! Or maybe two hundred.

What about you? What's your brand promise? What are you committed to delivering—every time? Whether you work for yourself or for someone else, you need to make a promise—and keep it. Be bold, be passionate, be unique. What do you provide that no one else could? What distinguishes you—or could distinguish you—from people who do similar things? How would you like someone else to describe you, in one powerful sentence? "Oh, yes," they'd say, "that's [your name] and she's the one who . . ." (You'll discover later how much I love having people complete that sentence.) And their words need to thrill you so that you think to yourself, *Yup, they've got that right. That's me. And nobody does it better.* Anything and everything that doesn't fit with that description is ripe for the throw-out bins—both mental and physical.

Green Tip: Old Ink and Toner

Everyone knows how easy it is to recycle paper, but what about other office supplies, like ink and toner cartridges? A company called Cartridge World (www.cartridgeworldusa.com) will actually pay you for the empty cartridge or refill it for a fraction of the cost of a new one. There are convenient locations all over the country.

Remember, *clutter blurs clarity.* Clutter also cramps your ability to be agile, not to mention your ability to spot the opportunity to periodically refine and at times, depending on market conditions, reinvent your brand.

Beth Comstock is a good friend, and she's definitely someone who knows the essence of her own particular brand. She defines herself as a change agent. She's truly brilliant at stirring innovation and change in whatever arena she finds herself. She has an uncanny ability to see new patterns: new ways to connect old seemingly disparate ideas into vibrant new wholes. For my money, that's the epitome of creative and strategic thinking. So for Beth to position herself as "operational" or "detail-oriented" or even "tactical" would be counter to her brand essence. It would blur or even totally obscure what makes her so unique.

A recent assignment required that she be a tactician. And because she's not only smart and totally committed to the corporation she works for, but a good team player as well, she tackled the assignment with her usual tenacity and did an extremely good job. It would have been easy and quite tempting for her to continue down the operational path and move forward in her company or another;

heaven knows she could pull it off. But that's not truly who she is. And that's not what, in the end, distinguishes her from everyone else inside or outside her company. So she convinced her boss (who, happily, is an enlightened leader) to make her next assignment one that would take advantage of her inventive spirit and ability to foment change. When she took the new position, she changed office locations—something she's done numerous times in the past. But there still was a lot to throw out of her old office, and a few things to bring along as well.

"Every time I make a move," Beth says, "I vow never to accumulate so much stuff again. And then every move, there I am, sorting through things and thinking, *Why did I save this? What was I thinking?*" Do you have any of those little office gadgets and trinkets that people usually have in their offices? I do. Beth does. Or did. "Why would a grown woman," she said to me, "need a bird that chirps when someone enters the room?" Beats me.

"And," she continues, "did I really think those Bill Clinton Russian-style nesting dolls were so special? I remember an old colleague who collected windup figurines and mementos of hot dogs. That's the first thing I think about when I think of him. I mean, who wants to be remembered as the hot-dog guy?"

Books are one of Beth's biggest indulgences, and for this move she finally went through and culled all the books that she could do without. (Actually, she found three—count them, three—boxes of books that had never

even been opened. They didn't make the cut.) "Look,"
Beth says, "I love books. They fuel my curiosity, and
maybe I think they symbolize who I am to my colleagues.
Surrounding myself with books shouts, *I want to learn. I am
a curious person. I am smart.*" But Beth decided that maybe she
no longer needed to make that point—and that in some
cases, her overabundance of books actually weighed her
down. "Books can be a burden and a source of frustration
because they remind me at every turn that I'll never have
enough time and energy to absorb what I've got, let alone
what's yet to be published."

Altogether, Beth let go of more than a dozen boxes
of books. (I told you she could teach us something about
books.) Some she forwarded to colleagues with notes about
why she enjoyed them and why they might like to as well
(a terrific idea); some were sent to the New York Public
Library. She also bought an Amazon Kindle (http://www
.amazon.com/Kindle-Amazons-Wireless-Reading-Device/
dpB000FI73MA), which can hold over two hundred
books and which she's using for her business and refer-
ence books, leaving her shelves to be filled with the vol-
umes that inspire and motivate her.

Beth's definitely a child of the Digital Age. Hey,
the *New York Post* didn't call her "the Digital Diva" for
nothing, but that's another story. She's committed to
going paperless and is filing everything electronically.
She recommends Google (www.google.com) and X-1 for
desktop search applications that, she says, "let you find

every e-mail, document, or presentation based on a few keywords."

Of course, not everything's going. There's a box of stuff that has traveled everywhere with her starting with her very first job. "It's like my special treasure chest," she says. "There are photos, old pet projects, special letters, press clippings, things with sentimental value. Every time I move, I add to it and sometimes I throw away things that no longer move me. I guess these things are a way for me to laugh at myself (usually at the crazy old hairstyles) or to say, *Atta girl*—and remind myself of those experiences and accomplishments that made me really proud."

By the way, it's good to have a box like that—as long as you know why you're keeping those particular things. If you can't figure that out, it's got to go.

Steps for clearing the clutter and clarifying your brand:

1. Decide who you are and who you aren't. Write down precisely what distinguishes you from people who do something similar—in your company or elsewhere. Declare your brand promise. Add these words to the end: . . . *and nobody does it better.* Be brave.

2. Throw out absolutely everything that either blurs or detracts from your brand—or drags you back to some old idea of yourself. Be brutal.

3. Consider going digital, as Beth recommends, and reducing the paper debris. Be thorough.

4. Don't spend a lot of time analyzing what worked and didn't work in the past. Let it go so you can live and work in the present. Be here now.

Gail's Throw-Out Scorecard:

22 old business guru books that I've never read

33 really old Lifedesigns presentation decks that don't reflect my current brand and drag me back into the past

Total: 2 things
Running Total: 37 things

Your Throw-Out Scorecard:

_____

_____

_____

_____

_____

_____

Your Total:
Your Running Total:

Chapter 9

Keeping What Works, Eliminating What Doesn't

I know a guy who has the room keys from every hotel he's ever been in during the last thirty years displayed on a wall. Seriously, there are keys from swell places—like the Ritz in London and the Hotel du Cap in Cap d'Antibes on the Riviera—but also not-so-fancy places like the Holiday Inn Express in Pittsburgh and the Days Inn in Tallahassee. Some of the memories they conjure up are good; some are bad. But good or bad, there they are. "Why do you keep all this stuff?" I asked him. "I don't know," he said. "I've been collecting it for a long time. I like looking at it."

It's okay to keep things around us, even in our offices, that give us pleasure—that we just like looking at. I don't think I could make it through a day in my office if I didn't have pictures of Jim, Kate, Abigail, and Willa to look at—and show to everyone who comes in. **But if something weighs you down or makes you feel bad, if it makes you tired, or keeps you from getting aloft in your life or your work, it's got to go.**

Speaking of what's got to go, Kathy Robb was looking around her office the other day while we were talking on the phone and spotted a bunch of baseball caps from various office outings—another example of "forced fun," right? One cap in particular caught her eye. "Oh, my God," she said, "that baseball cap really depressed me." Kathy's an environmental lawyer and has to make frequent site visits to conduct environmental audits. One particular trip was a nightmare. Her young daughter had the flu and Kathy hated being away from her even for an hour, never mind three days. To make matters worse, a blizzard delayed her flight home by a whole day. Needless to say, she was miserable. The baseball cap had been in the goody bag provided by the host company; when she got back to her office, she'd just plopped it on the shelf along with all the others. "You know," she said, "I almost feel sick looking at this thing." At that point, she put me on hold, walked over to her bookcase, grabbed the cap, and threw it into the wastebasket. "Wow, that feels good," she said when she got back on the phone. (Just for the record, Kathy later took the cap out of the wastebasket and placed it in the proper office recycling bin. I mean, she *is* an environmental lawyer, you know.)

The work–life balance issue plagues everybody I work with, both men and women—and stuff in the office that reminds any of us of those times when it seemed all work and no life really depresses us.

Scott Preiss is a highly effective executive in a financial institution but for his money, what makes him a worthwhile person is his absolute dedication to his family and to being there for them every single chance he gets. He's been to some pretty exotic places on business—Moscow, Tunisia, London, Beijing—and by his account never saw any of the wonders these cities had to offer. While his colleagues extended their trips so they could do some exploring, Scott never did. "My approach is, get in and get out," he says. "I'll do anything to get to the dinner table—the last vestige of American family communication and bonding—as soon as humanly possible, so I can hear the high and low points of each of our children's days. So I can be present for them." *What a guy*, you're thinking, right? Wait till you hear this: "To be honest," Scott says, "my heart is always heavy during these trips. Seeing incredible wonder or having extraordinary adventures without my amazing wife and four children is simply, to me, an empty feeling." And if you could have seen his face when he told me that, you'd have known he meant every word.

So what does Scott do to help purge the memories of some of these work–life imbalances? "Each December, I religiously gather the previous year's color-coded folders that represent the many days and hours of global negotiations, conflict, and sometimes resolution—and what I see isn't the positive impact I had, but rather the disappointment I feel from missing the dinners, smiles, hugs, and heart-filling conversations. So every year I pounce on these files—too important to destroy, too painful to keep—and I ship them off to archives with a satisfied smile. As the boxes leave my office, I feel at least some of the frustration about the folly of work–life balance fades away."

Okay, so most of us don't have an archives department to ship the too-important-to-destroy, too-painful-to-keep stuff to, do we? But we've got our attics and our garages, if necessary—where, with the proper containers and labels, we can get this stuff out of our eyesight and even out of our hearts. We've got to do it. Not doing it saps our energy big-time.

Important documents that you just don't want to look at but that shouldn't be thrown out can be put totally out of your sight by digitizing them. The same goes for important life documents that you're afraid you might lose or misplace at the exact moment you want to put your hands on them. Boy, aren't we glad we live in the Digital Age? Well, not all the time. But at this moment, it feels really good.

A Better Shredder

You'll probably want to shred most of your sensitive documents. It's also a good way to get out some of your aggression—seriously! (Try it if you don't believe me.) How do you know what kind of shredder to buy? There are two major kinds:

- A strip-cut model shreds your papers into long, thin strips. You'll need a larger basket to catch the strips, but the machine can handle high volume well without a lot of maintenance.
- A cross-cut version shreds vertically *and* horizontally to create confetti that would be difficult for anyone to piece back together. The shreddings compress a lot easier, so they won't take up as much room, but cross-cut shredders tend to cost more and require more maintenance.

Pat Perkins, who sells real estate in a lovely old town in Connecticut, really has the letting-go thing down. I think her attitude will inspire you to take another look around and do some more tossing. "Our generation," she says—meaning us fast-aging baby boomers—"has a particular need to collect stuff. Maybe because our parents, who went without and rationed their way through World War II, were savers, we've learned through observation that things are supposed to have value. The kids today are disposers—if it breaks, is worn, isn't up-to-date, they throw it out and start over."

Well, Pat's not a kid, but she sure is good at starting over and not looking back. "I've never had a problem leaving one profession for another and gleefully throwing things out with the changeover." Her husband, Rod, she points out, is the opposite. "He still has a huge bronze sign from the facade of a bank where he was once president. Why?" But Pat answers her own question: "I think it's harder for important people to let go of their old work stuff than it is for the regular Joe, like me," she says.

"For me, people who live solely on their laurels and accomplishments from the past are a yawn. I don't want to hear how wonderful you were in high school or how you used to bicycle twenty miles a day. I want to know: What are you doing with your life today? Looking backward holds no charm for me. What's done is done. Learn from it and move on."

See what I mean? Pat's a pistol, as we used to say in Ohio. She knows what's important and what's not—at least from her perspective. And if you met her, you'd be knocked out by her clarity, energy, and optimistic spirit. There's something to learn here: Whether you are—or were—a VIP or a regular Joe, let the old stuff go. How else will you have room and energy to reinvent and re-create yourself? "I like change and am ready for the next big adventure," Pat says, "which is how I see life—as a series of adventures." No wonder people like to hang out with her.

Interesting about Pat's observation that it's really hard to let go of the old office stuff when you're a VIP, or a big deal. A friend and client named Martha Gilliland had to work really hard to achieve that particular letting-go.

Martha is an intellectual, a true academic, a scientist. Her ultimate dream was to go the full distance, to become a respected scientist and the president of a public university who would lead a transformation of the educational experience for students. In her early sixties, she concluded that she had gotten as far as she was going to get in achieving those dreams—a respected but not famous scientist and a respected university president, one who had led her university partway, but not all the way, toward the transformation she envisioned.

So she's decided to let go of all the material from those years of achievement and struggle, including many of her scientific papers, even her awards and plaques. Oh, she's not tossing them into the garbage; she's boxing them and labeling them for her grandchildren. And on the spur of the moment, she went to Best Buy and bought a scanner so she could organize all her papers and pictures electronically. As she sifted through all these documents, she said, "I was shocked, overcome with emotion, even paralyzed at times. It was almost as if I were seeing them for the first time. And for the first time, I actually saw how good they were." Martha told me she said out loud, "Hey, this stuff is good! How did I do it? Gee, I was a real scientist, wasn't I?" But the idea of finally letting go of her old dream once and for all terrified her. "If I'm not going to be that person, if I'm not going to have that big title, that big office, that fame, who am I going to be?" she asked herself. Finally, after all the sifting and re-reading, after the packing and the scanning, Martha came up with the answer. "I'm going to be free," she said.

Does Not Compute

Have you recently upgraded your computer system? What to do with the old one? If it's still in working order, after you've removed all of your personal files, why not donate it to a local senior center? If it's broken, bring it to your local Staples store. For a ten-dollar fee, they will disassemble it and see that the parts are recycled properly.

Eddie Brill, a brilliant stand-up comic (I've got a little bit of a thing for stand-up comics) and the warm-up guy for the *Late Show with David Letterman,* let's go of the past just about every day. "I mean, I don't even keep videos of my best performances," Eddie says. "When they're done, they're done. I don't have room for nostalgia; I'm living in the now." Eddie believes that his ability to let go of his "old" work makes it much easier to relate to every new audience he comes in contact with. "I've got to under-stand them—who they are as individuals, what they need, how they're unique—if I'm going to move them. There's no time for worrying about what worked or didn't work in the past. There's only now." I agree with Eddie. The more stuff you surround yourself with, especially from your past work life, the less likely you are to actually connect with people who are important to you now. There's just not enough room. Think about that the next time you move that stack of papers from the right side of your desk to the left, will you?

Steps for keeping what works and eliminating what doesn't:

1. Take a look around your office at the tchotchkes, widgets, mementos, photographs, wall hangings—even the container you keep your pens and pencils in—and ask yourself if it weighs you down or gives you loft. If it's the former, you know what to do.

2. Consider tossing or storing your old plaques and awards from past positions. We don't have enough time or energy to look back. We already know what's old; our job is to discover what's new.

3. For those things that are too important to destroy, too painful to keep, put them in boxes with labels and place them in your attic, garage, or storage facility. Or digitize them. But get them out of your sight.

4. When you're finished dumping all this stuff, ask yourself the question, "Who am I now?" And answer with a clear voice, "I'm free."

Gail's Throw-Out Scorecard:

3 old manuscripts from past books. (They're digitized, plus I have actual books!)

Dozens of hard copies of agreements with corporations for workshops, speaking engagements, coaching assignments, et cetera. They're all digitized, too!

7 mementos from fun-filled corporate events, from canvas tote bags to plastic paperweights.

Total: 3 things
Running Total: 40 things

Your Throw-Out Scorecard:

_____

_____

_____

_____

_____

_____

Your Total:
Your Running Total:

Chapter 10

The Phoenix Rises from the Ashes

I t doesn't seem fair, but sometimes all our stuff has to be ripped away from us for us to let go . . .

David Hoffman is a documentary filmmaker—one of the best—and he has spent a forty-plus-year career "recording stories," as he puts it, about what he calls, "extraordinary/ordinary people." His reality films—more than 125 of them—have been broadcast on prime-time PBS, Turner Broadcasting, the Discovery Channel, and A&E. His stories have featured not only people like Ronald Reagan, Earl Scruggs, B. B. King, Bob Dylan, Joan Baez, and Jimmy Carter, but also people you've never heard of and, thanks to David, will never forget.

David lives and has his studio in the town of Bonny Doon, California, at the top of the Santa Cruz Mountains, in what is known as Big Tree Country. One morning not long ago, he'd left his house at the crack of dawn to drive to a meeting in the Silicon Valley over the mountains. At about 6:30 a.m., his wife, Heidi, called, screaming on his cell phone to tell him their house and

David's studio were on fire. She'd just called 911, grabbed their young sons, and run out of the house to warn neighbors. David drove back up the mountain at 120 miles an hour watching the smoke rise in the sky above the area where they lived. The four-alarm fire drew fifty firefighters, who did everything they could to save the house and studio. The house, at least the shell of it, survived; but David's studio—containing everything he'd created during his entire career as well as all the projects he was currently working on—burned to the ground. His film library and the original footage from forty-three years of work, his eight Emmys and other film awards and medals, his working documents, thirty-eight thousand pounds of data that had traveled with him through twelve different moves, everything, truly everything, was lost, all burned to ash in just minutes.

At first, David was devastated. He sat down crying in the smoldering rubble and thought, *There must be something I can salvage from this.* He and his daughter, Jeannie, and their neighbors who had been watching from a distance, started to dig. David invited everyone they knew to dig with them. "We attacked the debris like mad people," David said. "We pulled out negatives and prints by the thousands, all burned around the edges; we couldn't even tell what films they were from. It was all gone. My entire creative history and the only financially relevant legacy I had to leave my wife and three children were completely destroyed."

But David Hoffman is an optimist. "You know, I've never made a depressing or negative film. I make films about the glory of life, about what is triumphant. About the greatness of people. And I knew that whatever I made of this tragedy would be the creative statement that defined me. I had a choice: I could choose to come to a dead stop—or I could choose to keep going. I chose to keep going."

This truly was his defining moment: "I decided I had a new chance, a chance to start over, to do my greatest work, a chance I never thought I'd have. The fire dies; the Phoenix rises. I decided that this could be a thrilling period, that I could actually create *new criteria* for what was important in my life." And here is his commitment: "A year from now," he told me, "I want to be able to say I would have chosen this fire."

So what do you choose? Do you choose to come to a dead stop, or to keep going? To surround yourself with the artifacts of your history—or delight in the possibilities of your future? You get to decide. Now, that's thrilling.

The single step for rising from the ashes:

1. *Know this: Your greatest work is ahead of you.*

Gail's Throw-Out Scorecard:

I will throw out the middle-of-the-night fear that the future couldn't possibly be as good as the past.

Total: 1 thing
Running Total: 41 things

Your Throw-Out Scorecard:

_____

_____

_____

_____

_____

_____

Your Total:
Your Running Total:

Now that we've gone through your house and your office, I bet you've accumulated a terrific list of throw-outs! Log on now to www.throwoutfifty things.com to keep track of your progress and celebrate how far you've come! Now it's on to the emotional clutter! Don't forget to send us your pictures and videos so we can see what you've thrown out!

⁜

PART THREE

Attacking the Mental Mess

IF YOU THINK YOU CAN SEPARATE THE PHYSICAL FROM THE MENTAL CLUTTER, FORGET ABOUT IT!

You've already realized, I'm sure, how closely connected the physical and mental clutter are to each other. It's hard to throw out even something as innocuous as an old, beat-up bath mat without throwing out some old point of view of yourself with it. I know, I threw out an old bath mat recently; I could've kept it, it was still usable—like those old lipsticks that are worn so far down that the metal *casings* scrape your lips—and part of me thought, *Hey, it's not completely shredded, maybe you should hang on to it. I mean we're trying to economize here.* But it just didn't look good enough—didn't match my idea of the kinds of things I should surround myself with or, for that matter, put my bare feet on. I know you know what I mean. A good friend of mine believes that there are no items in your surroundings that shouldn't be scrutinized based on the *How Does It Make Me Feel?* scale. For example, she has a rule in her house that absolutely no wire hangers are allowed. When clothes come back from the cleaners on those hangers with the WE LOVE OUR CUSTOMERS signs on them, they're immediately tossed out or recycled and replaced with wooden or padded ones. "Wire hangers damage your self-esteem," my friend declares. "They're cheap and they make *you* feel cheap. Recycle them." I've taken her advice and so have my daughters. We all feel it perked us up a bit.

Now, those are just common, everyday, un-earth-shaking examples of the undeniable connection between physical and mental clutter. Here's a more dramatic example: A young woman I know named Kelly, recently divorced and determined to start her life all over—in a new town, with a new job, and hopefully a new set of friends—was in the thick of her Throw Out Fifty Things process. She was doing pretty well; it was easy to throw out many of the things that she and her ex had shared that either had never appealed to her or simply brought back a negative feeling. Until she got to her wedding pictures. And her wedding dress. "What should I do?" she asked. "I'm so done with that marriage. Or at least I'm trying to be . . ." She trailed off.

The fact was, Kelly was divorced, but she wasn't actually "done" with the marriage. There were moments when she'd wake up in the middle of the night wondering what she'd done wrong, wondering if it were all her fault, wondering if she should've worked harder at making her marriage work. (Just for the record, I cringe when someone tells me she's "working at" her marriage. I see an image of her out in the street with a crane, a crew of workmen, and a hard hat. But that's just me.) Anyway, Kelly had looked really beautiful in that wedding dress, and it had been an incredibly happy day. You could tell from the pictures that she was very much in love and no doubt expected to stay that way. And she did, for four years. And she might have felt that way for a whole lot longer except that she began to perceive that her husband, Brad's, idea of integrity—what was right and what was wrong—was so very different from hers that she found herself being angry at him or disappointed in him almost every day.

"You could sum up his personal credo," she said, "as this: If nobody finds out about it, it's okay. If everybody else does it, it's okay. If there's money to be made, or fame to be had, and I can get away with it, it's okay." Evidently, he was involved in some pretty shady dealings. He made quite a bit of money, hadn't gotten caught, and was very proud of himself. In fact, she said, he'd become arrogant, entitled, and had even begun to swagger. Kelly said, "I know it sounds funny but when he touched me, I actually began to feel myself recoil."

The day everything came apart was when Kelly discovered that Brad had cheated a mutual friend of theirs out of his fair share of a business transaction they had completed together. It turned out that Brad had forged the contract and lied about the actual numbers. The friend had trusted Brad, and although he was mystified about why the deal had netted out so much less than he'd expected—and although he'd counted heavily on the money to pay back a debt he owed—he didn't question Brad and accepted his word as truth.

Kelly was appalled. When she confronted Brad, he became enraged and told her she just didn't understand how things "were done." And to "get over it." "I wondered," she said, "if he'll do something like this, what *else* will he do? Will he cheat *me*? Will he cheat *on* me? Do I want to bring up my children with the belief that anything goes?" She told Brad the following day that she couldn't stay in the marriage any longer. He said, "Fine with me. I can't imagine being married to someone who's so stupid and incredibly naive."

So there we were with a gorgeous wedding dress and beautiful pictures. "Well, are you done with this marriage or aren't you?" I asked. "I don't think you can have it both ways." "That dress was really expensive," Kelly said with a frown. "You can sell it," I told her. "What about the pictures?" she asked. "You can either burn them or give them to your mom. Up to you. There are some nice shots of your family. What do you think?" She took a deep breath and said, "Burn 'em. I'm done with Brad, done with feeling bad, and done with being pulled back into a past that made me forget how bloody *good* I am. *Done!*" she said. "*Done!*" I said. Luckily, Kelly had a fireplace in her apartment, so we built a fire and threw the pictures in it. Then we called a consignment store and made arrangements to drop off the dress. Done.

What are some things in your life that are "over"—a job, a relationship, or maybe just a friendship—but not "done"? When something's not done it can haunt us, drag us back into the past, make us feel inadequate, angry, bitter, you name it, but it's not good. So the question is, what do we have to let go of to make it done? Maybe it's physical stuff, maybe it's mental stuff, maybe it's both.

The fact is that, until Kelly burned the pictures and threw out the dress, some vestiges of her failed marriage still haunted her. She still felt bad; still felt that maybe she should have worked harder at the relationship, that if she had, maybe she could have changed Brad. That word from my childhood, *hoshmahoken,* comes to mind again. "Nonsense," a more refined person might say. It's just not true. It was time for Kelly to let go of the regret, the anger, and the feeling of inadequacy so she could move on and create a new vision for the next drop-dead, never-been-so-good-before part of her life.

And that leads us into the next part of the Big Letting-Go: rounding up and throwing out the mental clutter. So in the next few chapters we'll be taking a look at some of the old habits or beliefs that we've held on to for years, maybe for decades, that slow us down—or in some cases stop us dead. **When we throw out the physical clutter, we clear our minds.** *When we throw out the mental clutter, we clear our souls.* And we need both of those vital parts of our being to be in good working order as we move into the next—and greatest—segment of our lives. So get ready for the Really Big Letting-Go.

Let's review the Rules of Disengagement and apply them to getting rid of the mental clutter:

One. If *it*—the belief, the conviction, the memory, the

mind-set or even the person—weighs you down, clogs you up, or just plain makes you feel bad about yourself, throw it out, let it go, move on.

Two. If it (see above!) just sits there, occupying precious mental space, backing up vital emotional arteries, and contributing nothing positive to your life, throw it out, let it go, move on. If you're not moving forward, you're moving backward; throwing out what's negative helps you discover (and make room for) what's positive.

Three. Don't make the decision—whether to toss it or keep it—a hard one. If you have to weigh the pros and cons for too long or agonize about the right thing to do, throw it out.

And remember, don't be afraid. This is your life we're talking about. The only one you've got for sure. You don't have time to waste on emotional or psychic waste.

Get out your notebooks and your pens, or your *Throw Out Fifty Things* workbook, because if it were ever important to write down what you're letting go of, *it's now*. You might not have an actual Hefty bag to throw your old convictions in, Goodwill might not be interested in them, and they might not fetch all that much on eBay, but the *value to you* in letting go of them is priceless. Here's the thing: We might weigh the pros and cons about whether or not to keep our old rugs, lamps, or china for our children, but when it comes to our old negative assumptions, our fears, our regrets . . . I mean, do we really want to pass that stuff on to the people we love best? (We really do pass on what we model, don't we?) And what tag or garage sale will have a table with a tent card that says "Old Insecurities, Fears, Mistakes and Regrets for Sale—Half Price! Get Them While They're Hot!" Probably not that many. Although, when you think about it, it's not a bad idea. Because if you write them down and give them up, they're done. So how about when you have your garage or tag sale (see "Sally Carr's 'Good Stuff' Tag Sale," in chapter 7), you provide a pencil, a pad of paper, and a big bowl, then invite people to write down and dump all their Mental Throwaways? You can have a small bonfire at the end of your sale with all those scraps of paper, and celebrate the letting-go of the mental and emotional junk from everyone's lives. What do you think? It might make your garage sale the most talked-about—and important—event of the season. Hey, it worked for Kelly.

And listen, the good news is that every single mental throw-out counts. If you throw out fifteen, it's fifteen. There are no multiples to worry about here. So heave ho!

Chapter 11

Letting Go of Feeling Inadequate, Irrelevant, and Just Plain Not Good Enough

This is a really good place to start the mental throw-out process, because who among us has not felt at one time or another (like maybe now) that we're just not good enough? I can tell you that without exception, among the individuals I've worked with—from women in homeless shelters to CEOs, from kids in college to college presidents, from the super-rich to folks wondering every day how to make ends meet—there isn't a single individual who hasn't felt that way.

Does that surprise you? Did you think you were the only one who wonders how in the world you've gotten as far as you have? And what in the world you're going to do to get any farther? Well, welcome to a wonderful club of terrific people. In fact, I'd go so far as to say that the very best people I know—and I'd define *best* as those people, like you, who are out to make a positive difference in the world and want to bring their best selves into a future of their own design—feel incredibly inadequate at one time or another in any given month, week, or even day.

Well, we're going to change all that. You, I, any one of us, are so much better, so much more powerful, so much more necessary to the workings of the world than we can imagine. You know that old saying, "No one's indispensable"? Well, I believe that *no one is dispensable.* When we allow ourselves to be, we're all vital to the positive outcome of whatever effort we involve ourselves in. Why don't we just get it about ourselves? And for the record, other people will never get it about us until we get it about ourselves. Funny how that works.

Have you ever said to yourself, *Since I don't know everything, I don't know enough?* There's a big difference between not knowing everything and not knowing enough, isn't there? Few people have been clearer about that than a very smart guy named Albert Einstein. Can you imagine where the world of physics would be if Einstein had decided that since he could never know it all, there would be no point in trying to know anything? There were some things at which Einstein was absolutely brilliant: seeing new patterns, connecting disparate dots into reasonable, workable wholes, for example. And other things about which he hadn't a clue. Legend has it that when he got on a bus, he'd simply hand the bus driver a bunch of change and ask him to take whatever was the right amount, because he couldn't figure it out himself.

Okay, I'm no Einstein (hey, maybe I *am* in some ways, how do I know for sure?), but I can figure out the change thing—sort of. But here's the point: He concentrated on what he *could* do and took energy from the doing of it. He didn't allow his energy to be depleted by what he couldn't do, didn't know—or what was just difficult or uninteresting to him. Many of us don't do that. We shine the spotlight *not* on what we can provide, but what we're missing. No wonder we feel inadequate. Don't do it. It's a ridiculous waste of energy, not to mention a waste of valuable mental resources that could be applied to creating the next Theory of Relativity. So when the *I just don't know enough to make a contribution* voice sounds off in your head, silence it . . . throw it out.

Here's a story that might bring the point home for you: A really lovely girl, someone I went to school with, actually, was extraordinarily creative. Her name was Olivia. She was more musical than anyone I'd ever met. She was not only an accomplished pianist, but she could compose music as well. She was a fine artist. Her drawings and paintings were exquisite; they reminded my woefully untrained eye of the French impressionist school. Olivia's mother was proud of her daughter's talents but in a moment of what possibly might be thought of as well-meaning criticism, she said, after viewing one of Olivia's paintings, "It's lovely, darling, but you'll never be Monet."

Olivia put down her brushes and didn't pick them up again for decades. She concluded that if she wasn't going to be as good as Monet, there was no use in painting at all. At the time, it didn't occur to her that she might have been meant to be a different kind of painter, that she could develop her own style, maybe even her own school. And it didn't occur to her that even if her works were never displayed in the Louvre or the Metropolitan Museum, they might have brought her joy just to paint them—and perhaps others might have found joy in just looking at them.

Luckily, Olivia grew up and, eventually, realized that being good enough was a totally meaningless and irrelevant concept. "Good enough for what?" she ultimately asked. "For whom?" For her mother's approbation? If most of us waited for that final seal of approval before we stepped forward in life, we might find ourselves stuck at the starting gate when the gun goes off. Let go of the phrase *as good as.* Throw it out. And while we're at it, let's let go of the ongoing and frequently overwhelming tendency we all have to compare ourselves with other people. You know what I mean.

Recently, Jim and I were driving home from a party and I asked, "So how did I look?" "Great," he said. "No, I mean really," I went on, "did Karen look younger? She's got great arms. I mean, seriously. How did I look?" Jim, as you've figured out by now, is an incredibly patient guy, not to mention a long-suffering one. He's surrounded by women. Even the canine, Willa, needs constant affirmation that she's a good girl. So he sighed and answered, "Really, you looked wonderful. Even, I mean especially, your arms. Honest."

It's ridiculous, isn't it? This comparing thing has to go. We start comparing ourselves at an early age—and more often than not we come up short in the process. I remember coming home from some little party when I was a girl and my grandmother saying, "Well, did you see anybody you liked better than yourself?" I replied in my serious twelve-year-old way, "Yes, I did. Margaret's smarter, Ina's prettier, and Suzy's taller." My grandmother said that she was just joking and that the question was simply an old Irish expression and was not meant to be taken seriously. "Oh," I said. "Well, anyway, they are."

When was the last time you fell into the comparisons trap? Last week? Last night? The habit is exhausting and deserves to go on the throw-out list. Write it down there right now. This is one of those things we're going to have to concentrate on every day if we're going to conquer it. There are so many opportunities to compare ourselves unfavorably. Almost every magazine we pick up, every commercial we see, invites us to check out how we stack up against somebody else—in terms of income, education, health, our bodies, our homes, our children, even the vacations we take, the food we serve, the clothes we wear, and the cars we drive. No wonder we fall for it. But it's got to stop. And this is the day to stop it.

Review this statement every morning: *I will not compare myself with others, nor them with me. I will appreciate myself and others for what I and they contribute.*

The point isn't whether or not I'm Einstein or Monet, or even Posh Spice. The point is that I am living now and that I have precious gifts to give and precious time to give them. So I'll give them now. Period.

Are you thinking of something right now that could be really, really hard for you to let go of? I am—and I need to get it off my chest.

I told you about my brother, Jay, in chapter 7 when I discussed unpacking his marvelous paintings that had been stored in my garage for years. As you recall, my family and I lost Jay, a navy pilot, my senior year in college when his fighter jet crashed into the Mediterranean. He was twenty-four years old. We were an incredibly close family, and Jay was not only my hero but my best friend. I would have given my life for him . . . and I've been angry for a long time because I wasn't given the chance. I thought if one of us wouldn't be allowed to make it, for one reason or another, it would and should have been me. It's not that I undervalued myself, it's just that I valued Jay so highly. It's not that I feel I haven't made contributions to the world, I've just always thought his contributions would have been much greater. And right now, as I've been writing this chapter, it occurs to me that I need to let go of comparing who I am with what my brother might have been. And that I need to finally, after all these decades, let go of the anger I've felt for not being able to give my life in exchange for his. It will be hard. But it's time to do it. So I will.

If you've got some old inadequacy that still haunts you, still weighs you down and makes your heart heavy, this is the time to let it go. And you can do it. We can do it together.

Steps to help you let go of needless negative comparisons and dump debilitating feelings of inadequacy:

1. Let go of the old adage "No one's indispensable." No one's *dispensable.* Everyone counts. Whatever you can contribute is valuable. Give what you can every chance you get.

2. Let go of thinking that you need to know about or be good at everything. Celebrate what you do know. Enjoy what you can do. Remember Albert Einstein.

3. Don't fall into the trap of thinking that to make a big difference you have to make it in the big time. Some of the most significant contributions in the world—or in your town—have been made by people who never had their work displayed at the Louvre, never appeared on *American Idol,* and never were interviewed by Larry King.

4. Don't compare yourself with others. It's childish and pointless. You be you and let others be whomever and whatever they are. Be happy for someone else's good day or good fortune—so they can be happy for yours. And most of all, be happy that you're here now—and that you have the chance to give your own unique gifts to the world.

Gail's Throw-Out Scorecard:

I will let go of comparing what I've contributed to the world with what my brother would have contributed had he lived.

Total: 1 thing
Running Total: 42 things

Your Throw-Out Scorecard:

_____

_____

_____

_____

_____

_____

Your Total:
Your Running Total:

Chapter 12

Letting Go of the Type of Person You Think You Are— or Aren't

I wish I had a dollar, or even a dime, for all the people who have told me that they're just not the type to do something they want to do or act in a way they'd like to act. For example, have you ever heard yourself say something like this: "I'm not the type to go up to people I don't know and introduce myself. I'm the shy type. Always have been." And all of us say things like that with absolute conviction—like we're reciting the gospel—like that's the way it is and that there's absolutely no changing it. "It is what it is" is a statement we hear almost daily.

Well, I'm not so sure there's *any* way it is. Did you ever see that marvelous film *Becket*? Richard Burton plays Thomas à Becket, the Archbishop of Canterbury who was murdered and later canonized under the rule of Henry the Second, king of England. Henry is played by one of my favorite actors, Peter O'Toole. There's a stunning scene on a beach where Thomas and Henry meet on horseback for what is to be their last conversation. Henry is explaining to Thomas why the rule of the Crown is final and unquestionable in all things—including those things relating to the Church of England and to all religious questions in general. "Don't you see, Thomas," Henry says, "it is written." Whereupon Thomas replies, "No, it is not written until it is written *here*." And he touches his finger to his temple to make his point. This, to me, is the pivotal moment in the film. It brilliantly clarifies the fundamental and irreconcilable difference between the two men. One believes that "it is what it is"; the other believes that only the individual decides what it is. I'm with Thomas. I believe that at any given moment we can decide who we are, what we stand for, what we're capable of, and what type we are. And that means that at any given moment, we can throw out the old type if it just doesn't work for us.

But the fact is, we typecast ourselves into a corner starting at an early age. Or someone else does.

My mom, who gave me some of the best and bravest advice in the world, also typecast me into a little tight box with the label DISORGANIZED, didn't she? Doesn't make her any less spectacular and wise as a mother, just makes her human. The typecasting thing is an ever-present danger for all of us, believe me. We do it to ourselves and we do it to our own children. I heard myself tell Abigail a few days ago that she was the "creative type." Now, creative is a good thing to be, right? And she's definitely creative. But she's not a type. And by typecasting her, I could give her the impression that I thought she *wasn't* other things—like operational, logical, practical, and, uh, organized. And that wouldn't be at all true. But if she made that deduction and believed it, it would seem true to her. (Don't worry, she doesn't think that. She takes most of what I say with a grain of salt, and her optimistic soul usually puts the best possible spin on it. Still, it's good to watch oneself.)

But I bet if I asked you right now what type you are, you could tell me with ease. Okay, I'm asking you. And I can hear you say, "I'm the right-brain type." Or "I'm the sensitive type," or "I'm the not-good-at-math type," or "I'm just not the athletic type," or as one woman named Peg declared recently, "Gail, I'm just not the morning type. I hate getting up early and I'm just no good until the afternoon." Now, this woman had gotten into a bit of hot water at her job, as you can imagine, given the fact that her boss was very much the morning type and did not take kindly to Peg's coming in late—religiously.

"So, when did you first get it that you weren't the morning type?" I asked. "Oh, I've just always known it," Peg said. "Well, today we're going to make up a new type for you, Peg," I said. "Today we're deciding"—boy, I love that word, *decide*—"that you're the energetic, loves-to-get-up-in-the-morning type. Today we're declaring that you can be any type you want to be, that you are the only one in charge here, and that *it is not written until you write it.* Have you got it?"

"Hmmm," Peg said, "but what about my, uh, tendencies to be, you know, not sharp, not energetic in the morning?" "Sorry, you're just not that type any longer," I said. "We're done with it. It doesn't work for us. We're letting it go." Does that sound like just a whole bunch of wishful thinking to you? Well, it's not. Actually, Peg bought into her new type and played it to the hilt. My father always told me to "act the way you want to feel." That's what Peg did and, lo and behold, she turned into a morning person.

Now, I'm not saying Peg didn't have to work at letting go of her type. She did. Old mental habits are definitely hard to break. (You know that when I walk into my closet and it's got stuff all over the place, I have to fight saying, *See, Gail, you'll never be as organized as your mom,* and instead just start straightening things up.) But Peg was energized by the realization that she was no longer held captive to a part she'd acted for years; that she could, at any given moment, recast herself into a new part. And she quickly learned that if she acted that part with enough conviction, she would convince herself and others that it was true.

Let's talk about conviction and acting for a minute. There was a young woman I once knew named Teri who was majoring in acting. In one of her workshops she was given an assignment to pick a soliloquy from a play by Shakespeare and present it to the class. Teri chose the final love scene from *Romeo and Juliet.* Now, a director would have been hard-pressed to cast Teri as Juliet. He'd probably think she just wasn't the type. She was short, on the pudgy side, and not your classic beauty by any stretch of the imagination. But Teri had something much more important than any of those qualities. She had conviction. She believed, without a shadow of a doubt, that she *was* Juliet. She saw herself as beautiful, desirable, innocent, and totally worthy of Romeo's adoration. And she acted accordingly. Teri amazed and thrilled the class. And when she finished, they gave her a standing ovation. Here's what she can teach us: *There is no way it is. There's only the way you say it is.* And if you say it and act it wholeheartedly, the audience—any audience—will buy it lock, stock, and barrel. Including that toughest of all audiences, the audience of one: you.

Right now, if we choose, we can throw out our old act and create an entirely new one. The ability to recast ourselves into a type that serves us rather than a type that sabotages us is at our fingertips. We just have to reach out and grasp that ability and use it. Are you thinking, *Oh, right, Gail, first of all, I'm no actor and second, I've been the way I am for decades and no short class in improvisation is going to change that. Give me a break.* Okay, I understand how you feel. But I know differently. I know that if you act the way you want to feel, you'll eventually feel that way—and, more importantly, *be* that way. Here's a story that will prove my point.

A number of years ago, I conducted a workshop for a group of women who lived in a homeless shelter on the outskirts of New York City. They were all in their twenties, many of them had children, and those who were married rarely, if ever, saw their husbands, because they were in jail. They were out of work, out of hope, and to a woman convinced that "that's the way it is"—in *this* life, anyway. One of the workshop participants, named Serena, was particularly sullen and angry. She slumped down in her chair, refused to look at the workshop facilitators, and wouldn't speak. She was dressed in men's clothes and wore a hat pulled down over her eyes. Serena, like virtually all the women in the workshop, was the victim of violence and ongoing physical abuse.

By the second day of the workshop, most of the women had loosened up somewhat and had begun to speak out loud and actually talk to one another—something they hadn't done even in the shelter. Eventually, Serena began to engage in our conversations as well. We began talking about the need to stand up for oneself, to refuse to assume that abuse and violence were just an automatic part of everyday life. Here's what Serena said: "You don't understand, Gail. *I'm the type person who gets abused.* If I was with another man, he'd abuse me, too. It's how it is with me. And it always will be." She wasn't alone in her conviction. Most of the other women nodded. That's how it was. "Who says?" I asked. "Where is it written that that's how it is? In the Bible? In a book you read at school? In the Constitution of the United States? Where? Show me!"

Well, as you can imagine, it took a lot more conversation, a lot of soul searching and not a few tears for these wonderful women to chisel their way out of the marble of their lives; to let go of their resignation and even consider that they might be able to create a different reality for themselves. And for Serena, the conversations created nothing short of a miracle. By the end of the workshop, she had retypecast herself. She went from a woman who cast herself as the type whom men abused, to a woman who cast herself as strong, bold, and powerful . . . a woman who decided and designed her life according to her own convictions. And a woman who, she declared, would be out of the shelter, employed, and caring for her children and on her own within six months. When Serena made that declaration to the workshop participants, she stood up, took off her hat, looked each person straight in the eye, and spoke in a clear voice. There wasn't a dry eye in the house.

Five months later, the phone rang in my office. A woman's voice said, "You don't know me, Miss Blanke, but I have a woman named Serena in my office whom I've just hired. She said I needed to call you and tell you she was one month early in her promise to you." "Her promise to herself, you mean," I said. "I knew she'd keep it." A few weeks later, Serena appeared in my office for a surprise visit. She was wearing a lovely dress, her hair was beautifully combed, she was standing up straight—and she was smiling. *That's what* proud *looks like,* I thought to myself. Everyone in the office gave her a standing ovation.

If Serena can recast herself, imagine what you can do.

So let go of the old type thing—throw it out once and for all, okay? You can recast yourself any day you want to. You and you alone get to decide and design who you are, what you're good at, and even how others perceive you.

Not Your Type?

Here's a list of some of the types people tell me they are or aren't. Take a look and ask yourself if you've fallen into any of these type traps. You can add some others to the list, by the way. Then decide which ones you're going to let go of. You should be able to come up with at least two or three things to add to your Mental Throw-Outs list. Maybe more. Go for it.

- I'm not the aggressive type.
- I'm not the salesman type.
- I'm not the corporate type.
- I'm not the entrepreneurial type.
- I'm not the political type.
- I'm not the operational type.
- I'm not the creative type.
- I'm not the type to get up in front of people and talk (90 percent of my clients tell me this).
- I'm not the athletic type.

- I'm not the type to wear fishnet stockings (somebody told me that yesterday).
- I'm the shy type.
- I'm the sensitive type.
- I'm the cautious type.
- I'm the can't-lose-weight type.
- I'm the can't-stop-smoking type.
- I'm the serious type.
- I'm the noncompetitive type.
- I'm the dull type.
- I'm the slow type.
- I'm the always-sees-the-dark-side type.
- I'm the self-sabotaging type (I hear this at least once a week).

Steps for letting go of the type of person you think you are—or aren't:

1. Make a list of the various types you think you are; types you or someone else made up that make you feel inadequate in some way and that you've accepted as the truth. Things like the can't-keep-her-mouth-shut type, or the not-good-at-math type, or the always-looks-at-the-dark-side type will pop up. Draw a line through every one of these words. Then write them on your Mental Throw-Outs list.

2. Write down some types you'd like to be; types such as confident, or charming, or unstoppable. Act as if you are those types.
3. Make up stories about yourself that please you, or embellish upon stories someone else has made up that you like. Think of yourself as that person. Actually, you *are* that person.
4. Remember, nothing's written until you write it.

Gail's Throw-Out Scorecard:

I will let go of thinking of myself as the not-organized type.

Total: 1 thing
Running Total: 43 things

Your Throw-Out Scorecard:

_____

_____

_____

_____

_____

_____

Your Total:
Your Running Total:

Letting Go of the Regrets and Mistakes of the Past

When Jimmy Durante was asked if he had any regrets, he allegedly said, "Millions. But luckily, I can't remember any of 'em."

We should all be so lucky. But for most of us, it's not the good stuff we remember, it's the regrets, the things we wished we'd done differently, the so-called mistakes we've made that we concentrate on. Actually, we don't just concentrate on them, we don't just wake up in the middle of the night chewing on them, no, we magnify them, we paint them in living color with the latest in high-definition technology, and then we hurl them at ourselves with the determination and zeal of an Olympic discus thrower.

Or am I the only one who does this? No, I couldn't be. If I were, we'd have come a heck of a lot further as a civilization. We'd have cured world hunger, created world peace, and discovered those other life-forms out there we've been looking for, wouldn't we? But it's hard to be truly brilliant or even just plain smart, not to mention fully engaged in a worthwhile or fulfilling pursuit, when we're paralyzed by the memories of all of our past screw-ups. (Forgive me, but *mistakes* seems like too tame a word in this context.)

I recently met a woman named Heide who told me she'd always been so afraid of failing that she only attempted those things in her life and career that she knew for sure she'd succeed at. "So you can imagine how limited my experiences have been so far," she said with a dry laugh. I guess you could say Heide's lucky, too, because sort of like Durante (but for different reasons), she has no major failures to regret. On the other hand, she has no stunning successes, either. Actually, she does have one regret: that she didn't push herself further, that she hadn't (at least not so far) had the thrill of risking everything for something, or even for someone she was passionate about. Not to worry: Heide and I are about to change that. We've decided that she's going to move it out; she's going to let go of her need to be certain of success and try some new, riskier things in her life. In fact, she's committed to having, of all things, a list of failures and mistakes to report back within six months. And along with it, I promise you she'll have some wonderful successes to report as well.

The point is: You can't succeed big-time if you're not willing to fail—big-time. The two go hand in hand; like peas and carrots, as Forrest Gump would say. We all know that. So why do we get so upset when we mess up? I think it's for two reasons. One: We have some dyed-in-the-wool notion that we have to be perfect—flawless, above any criticism or reproach. And two: We take all our failures and mistakes personally.

Well, not everybody. Michael Jordan doesn't. "I have missed more than 9,000 shots in my career," he says. "I have lost almost 300 games. On 26 occasions I have been entrusted to take the game's winning shot . . . and missed. And I have failed over and over and over again in my life. And that is why . . . I succeed." Worth remembering, isn't it?

Do you know how many times Madame Curie tried to turn pitchblende into radium and failed? Hundreds of times. She sifted through a ton of pitchblende before she was finally able to distill the tiniest amount of uranium. Was she momentarily disconsolate? Probably. Did she at any given moment consider *herself* a failure? I doubt it. She just kept going, kept trying, kept believing. And eventually, she succeeded.

And can you imagine how many times Fred Astaire, after he auditioned for a part in a movie, heard that awful word, "Next!"? Evidently, a zillion times. Boy, *next* is a hard word not to take personally. You've probably heard the story about how the notes from an MGM casting director were discovered where she'd written, after auditioning Astaire, "Can't sing; dances a little." Ouch! But he kept going—kept singing, kept dancing. It must have taken a lot of heart to burst out onto that stage when a bunch of people had told him his talent was mediocre to poor. It also must have taken a lot of passion for performing. Passion for the doing of something, passion for the end result—regardless of what it is—can get you through even the most dispiriting moments.

We've all messed up. We all have those middle-of-the-night moments (hours?) when we castigate ourselves for not knowing better, for not seeing it coming, for not trying harder, for not standing up for ourselves—or not keeping quiet for once, if that's what retrospect suggests. For not being perfect.

But perfectionism, like martyrdom, is highly overrated. Take a look at the people you like best, respect most, or just like to hang out with. Are they perfect? I doubt it. I bet they're wonderfully flawed people who have touched your heart because they came up short in one way or another and made a comeback. Even those who have made serious errors in judgment can re-earn our respect—and ultimately our forgiveness. Maybe even our love.

I know a man named Jack who was not only fired but actually escorted out of the building for taking bribes from one of his firm's suppliers. The incident wasn't exactly public knowledge, but word got around among people in Jack's industry and ultimately, among the circle of Jack's friends. Jack was devastated. He considered himself and his reputation ruined. I met him nearly nine months after the affair, and he was still distraught. "I don't know what I was thinking," Jack told me. "I guess I just *wasn't* thinking." I must say, Jack just wasn't the kind of guy whom you'd ever expect to lie, steal, or cheat to even the slightest degree. All his business and personal dealings had always been aboveboard and beyond reproach. "He's never even cheated on his income tax returns," his wife, Vicki, told me. "He was an Eagle Scout in high school, for heaven's sake." So how does someone that good get into that kind of trouble? The answer is: easy.

Here's what happened: Jack was responsible for arranging incentive reward trips for the top executives in his company and routinely dealt with travel companies who specialized in getting the best airfares and most luxurious accommodations. Jack's budgets for these trips were in the hundreds of thousands of dollars. One of the suppliers whom Jack had dealt with for years casually suggested that Jack and his wife should join him and his wife on a safari to Africa where the supplier would be scouting locations for an upcoming trip for another client. The cost of the trip (easily fifteen grand) would be on the house because they were such good friends. Jack accepted the offer, and the two couples had the trip of a lifetime—and the pictures to prove it. Jack and his wife actually renewed the closeness they'd felt at the beginning of their marriage thanks to the experience they shared.

"You know, in the back of my mind I knew it wasn't right," Jack said, "but it didn't seem all that wrong, either. I guess it just didn't seem like such a big deal at the time." Jack was close to tears. How many of us have done something that, in the back of our mind, we knew wasn't quite right? And somehow it didn't seem like all that big a deal at the time. Seriously, if you think about it, most of us have done a little something (or a not-too-little something) that we knew wasn't quite right. And as my grandmother was so fond of saying, "It's easy to get into trouble, but hard to get out."

"Okay, look," I said, "regardless of the way it might appear at the moment, this is not the end of the world. Did you make a mistake? For sure. Did you hurt anyone else? No, thank God. Is the mistake irrevocable? Not at all. Here's what we're going to do. We're going to throw out fifty things." Well, you can imagine Jack's reaction. "I'm sorry, Gail, but how the heck is that going to help?" he asked. "You'll see, my friend," I answered. I asked Jack to go through every room in his house and his home office and throw out anything and everything that no longer served him, closely following the Rules of Disengagement you and I discussed in the introduction.

Jack, like the good Eagle Scout he was, dutifully applied himself to his task. He surprised himself with all the physical debris he'd collected during the last few years. He'd been so busy working that he hadn't taken the time to let go of clothes he hadn't worn in a decade, books and CDs he no longer had a taste for, and even a bottle of aftershave that reminded him of the day he got fired. That was the last time he'd worn it. As he was rummaging around, he came across a folder with pictures of himself and Vicki on safari. It seemed like that was the last time they were happy. He told me he choked back tears as he called Vicki in to look at them. "Well, we're not throwing these out," he said, putting his arms around her. "In fact, I'm going out now to buy frames for them. These were good times."

That marked the turning point for Jack. In deciding to keep the pictures and celebrate the wonderful time he and Vicki had enjoyed together, he was able to begin to let go of the guilt he'd felt for nearly a year over the mistake he'd made. And once he could let go of the guilt, he could let go of the mistake itself. Oh, he didn't totally exonerate himself. There was no question in his mind that he should have acted differently. But it was done. And now it was time to begin to move forward. Jack made a list of all the good things he'd done in his life so far (Vicki helped him) and another list of all the things he regretted or wished he'd done differently. He put the GOOD THINGS list in a leather folder. He tore up the REGRETS list and threw it out. He was a free man. Free to recast himself as an accomplished, hardworking, reliable executive who, yes, sometimes learned things the hard way.

But he sure did learn 'em.

Jack has started an executive consulting business that concentrates on helping to prepare high-potential executives for high-risk roles. A major element of his curriculum is on the subject of—guess what? Ethics. It won't surprise you that Jack's programs are in high demand.

Why don't you make similar lists to the ones Jack made? It couldn't hurt. And add the GOOD THINGS list to your master list of THINGS I'M GOING TO KEEP and the REGRETS list to the master list of THINGS I'M THROWING AWAY.

Here's a nice story that's been circulating around some of the major financial institutions lately: A young investment banker, in his zeal to impress his boss, made a bad call that ended up costing his firm ten million dollars. The young man reported his mistake to the boss and said, "I'm sure you're going to fire me and I just want you to know, I don't blame you." "Fire you?" shouted the boss. "Why would I fire you? I've just spent ten million bucks training you."

One more story about mistakes. It's about one of the many I've made, and I made it at a pretty early age. It just goes to show you're never too young to start making mistakes, learning from them, and letting them go.

Halfway through the ninth grade, we moved from Cleveland to Toledo. It was a bit traumatizing, not only because I knew no one in my new school, but also because all my classes were more advanced than those in the school I'd left. Latin, especially, was a challenge. My new school used the same textbook, but the class was light-years ahead of where I was. Miss Sager was the Latin teacher and also dean of girls. She was a tough, no-nonsense disciplinarian, and the whole class both feared and respected her. She gave a Latin quiz every Wednesday.

I'd studied hard. I hadn't done very well on the past tests, and I was incredibly nervous. In the middle of the quiz, when I was stumped on yet another vocabulary word, I sneaked a glance at the test paper belonging to the girl sitting at the desk next to mine. Then I did the unthinkable: I copied the word off her paper. I handed in the test, and since it was the last class of the day, I went home. By the time I got home I was a wreck. The minute I saw my mother I began crying. Hard. "I've made a terrible mistake," I cried. "I cheated on my Latin test!" My mother put her arms around me and let me cry for a while and then she said, in her very wise way, "Well, what do you think you should do about it?" "I better go in tomorrow and tell Miss Sager," I said. "That sounds like a very good idea," my mom said. "Now, don't think about it anymore until the morning, promise?" I promised. And not surprisingly, I slept like a log that night. Nothing like a pending confession to lighten a girl's load.

I went into Miss Sager's office first thing in the morning and told her what I'd done. "Hmmm," she said, looking at my paper. "Which word did you take?" "That one," I said, pointing to the word I'd copied. "Well, you got it wrong, anyway," she said. "I'm really sorry," I said, trying not to cry. "I know you are," Miss Sager said. "But I have to give you an F on the quiz. Too bad, you wouldn't have done badly. But I'll tell you one thing, Gail," she continued. "When I look out at that class from now on, I'll know that of all the people in the room, there will be one person for sure who will never, ever cheat. And that one person will be you." It turned out to be one of the best days of my life.

Steps for letting go of your regrets and mistakes:

1. Remember, you gotta fail. It's the only way to succeed.

2. *Perfect* just isn't in the cards. A few pitchers have pitched perfect games; no one's pitched a perfect season. Throw out *perfect*.

3. Don't take your so-called failures personally. If something doesn't work, rejigger it and try it another way.

4. If you spend all your energy on reliving the things that didn't work, what you should or shouldn't have done, should or shouldn't have said, you'll have no energy for finding new ways to be fulfilled. Let that stuff go. That should be worth ten things on your list right there.

Gail's Throw-Out Scorecard:

I will throw out the slight but bothersome regret that I didn't become an actress.

Total: 1 thing
Running Total: 44 things

Your Throw-Out Scorecard:

_____

_____

_____

_____

_____

_____

Your Total:
Your Running Total:

Chapter 14

Letting Go of Being Right About How Wrong Everybody and Everything Is

I have the feeling we're on a roll now. I told you: Once you get going with the Mental Throw-Outs, there will be absolutely no stopping you. But if you still need some prodding, this chapter will do it for you. I promise.

There's not a single person I've ever worked with who didn't have a case of the "rights." You know what I mean; you've probably got a case yourself. Here's how to tell if you do: Have you heard yourself say out loud or to yourself in the last twenty-four hours, something on the order of: "Are you telling me that this plane isn't going to take off for another hour and a half, and you don't even know why? Do you realize I have a meeting to go to? That's just not right." Or "Why doesn't he ever remember that I always take milk in my coffee? After all these years, I don't get it; it isn't right." Or "Excuse me, we were here before those people, we should have been seated first! Do you know how long we've been waiting? That's not right." (Gotcha on that one, didn't I?)

Being right about how wrong someone or something is can be pretty irresistible for most of us. It's a trap we fall into on almost a daily basis. You can be right about how wrong your boss is to ignore how hard you've worked all year and offer such a small bonus. You can be right about how wrong your sister-in-law is to give you a too-small sweater for your birthday for the fourth year in a row. And you can be right about how your daughter should have just cleaned up the kitchen without having to be asked three times. And the thing is, you probably *are* right. And you probably could get a bunch of people to agree with you and you could all sit on a bench together and revel in your rightness. But then what? While you're busy being right, your whole life could float on by.

As a long holiday weekend approached last spring, I was chatting with a friend of mine about what each of us planned to do with our families. I had just finished getting through a busy travel schedule and was looking forward to hanging out with Jim and the girls and doing what we love best: planning what we're going to have to eat, cooking it, eating it, and then talking about how great it was. But my friend was of a different mind. She had a bad case of the rights. "Well, I'll tell you what my husband is going to be doing," she said. "He thinks he's going to play golf with his friends, but he's actually going to be taking down the Christmas lights outside our house. Do you know how many times I've asked him? It's almost summer, for heaven's sake. It's not right."

"You're right," I said.

"Of course I am," she snapped, "it's ridiculous."

"I know," I said, hesitating, "but I was just wondering . . ."

"Wondering what?" She really looked annoyed.

"I'm just wondering what kind of weekend you want to have."

"What do you mean?" She sounded suspicious.

"Well, I don't know. Maybe you'd like to have a cozy, romantic weekend together. I mean the children will be at friends' houses, right? And I just thought . . ."

"Go on," she said.

"Look," I told her, "you can be committed to being right about how wrong he is not to have taken down those blasted Christmas lights sooner, or you can be committed to having a really delightful weekend together. But you can't have both. A ticked-off guy usually isn't all that romantic, in my experience."

She thought for a minute. "Hmm, but what about all those lights? I'm so sick of them."

"It depends on what you want more," I replied.

Ultimately, my friend chose the romantic weekend with her husband, and because she was focused on making it delightful, it really was. And guess what? Her husband took down the Christmas lights without even being asked. (He didn't go golfing, either . . .)

Being right can, unfortunately, make you really unhappy. In fact, it can take over your life. On your Mental

Throw-Outs list, "being right" has got to be just about at the top. Here's an example of how the right thing almost ruined a woman's life:

Lauren is a highly successful woman who had a chronic case of the rights. She was very vocal about how right she was that her husband should be earning more money "at his age." She was right that her little daughter should have learned to walk "by now." She was endlessly right that the company she worked for was wrong to give her such a small salary increase every year, and finally she was right about how inept the people who worked for her were. Lauren actually might have been right on some counts, but boy, was she tough to be around. Her husband moved out for several months and came very close to leaving her for good. Her daughter almost never smiled, and there was so much turnover in her department that she missed out on a big promotion. Lauren, at her wit's end, finally asked me what I thought she wasn't doing right.

"Nothing you can't fix," I told her. "Then what?" she asked. "You just have to let go of one thing. And it's something we all need to let go of—the need to be right."

"Yeah, but how do I do that?" she asked. "It's sort of been my life—you know?"

I told Lauren that whenever she felt the need to be right about how wrong someone or something was, she should press PAUSE.

"Just take a few beats and ask yourself this question:

What am I committed to? Am I committed to being right about how far behind my daughter might be at any given moment, or could I be committed to something much greater, like creating a warm, positive environment, one that enables her to grow up with confidence and optimism? Am I committed to being right about how inadequate everyone who works for me is, or am I committed to creating an energetic, optimistic workplace where enthusiastic people devote their best selves to what they do every day?"

"So what do I do with the being-right thing?" she asked.

"You let it go," I said. "You throw it out. You go for the greater reward."

Well, Lauren had to practice pressing PAUSE like crazy—as I said, these mental habits are tough as anything to break—but she eventually licked it. And it changed her life, not to mention the lives of the people around her. Her husband's not only back, but feeling good about himself. Her daughter is running, jumping, and skipping like any little girl her age. And the turnover in Lauren's department has been cut in half. Lauren even looks different. The furrows between her eyes have all but disappeared. See? Letting go of being right is cheaper than a shot of Botox, and it lasts longer, too.

I catch myself being right all the time. Well, not all the time. Lots of times I don't catch myself, but luckily Kate or Abigail does. They call it "When Mom does *just a minute.*"

Abigail does a doozy of an imitation of me about when we were visiting her at school a couple of years ago. We had taken her out for dinner, and I called over the maître d' and said, "Just a minute, see that couple sitting at the bar right in front us? They're absolutely *all over* each other; it's disgusting. Can you please do something about it. It's not right." Abigail was mortified. But I've always done it. She should be used to it by now.

There was the time I raced to a salon as it was closing to pick up some much-needed hair gel and they wouldn't let me in, and I said, "Just a minute, do you realize I left work early to get here?"

Or—this was a good one—when Kate was eight years old and the mother of one of her friends invited a group of children to a slumber party but didn't invite Kate, I actually accosted the unsuspecting mother on a sidewalk in Manhattan and said, "Just a minute, it's not right not to invite everyone. You simply can't just leave one child out!" We laugh about it now, yet who knows how many battles I won and how many wars I lost? A lot, I'm afraid.

But I'm done with that. *Just a minute* goes out. Out, I tell you.

Take a look back into the last few months at the times you insisted on being right or did your own version of *just a minute.* Does it seem silly now, or are you still set on how right you were—and are? It's really easy to get good and stuck in a right groove.

We can get so focused on the small win, like Lauren, that we totally lose sight of what might have been a thousand times more important.

And that almost happened to a man I coached named, Jerry. Jerry's mom had abandoned him when he was a baby. She'd said she just couldn't cope with being a mother and moved to another state. Jerry was taken care of by his grandmother, who loved him dearly and tried to make up for the absence of his mom. Eventually, he grew up, was married, and had two children. Ironically, Jerry's wife left him and the children to go back to school several states away. Jerry was a wonderful father by all accounts, and he and his children became very close. Still, he'd never really gotten over the fact that his own mother had left him and how wrong that was. And now it had happened again—not only to him, but to his own children. And that was really wrong. Well, one day Jerry's wife returned and wanted to resume her relationship with their children. She said she'd changed, she'd grown up, and that she thought she could be a good mother.

Understandably, Jerry was angry. "It's just not right," he told me. "She left them. She never even visited them. She hasn't seen them for nearly five years. And now she wants to come back. Just like that."

"You're right, Jerry," I said quietly, "no one would argue with that." Jerry didn't say anything for a long time. You could see him wrestling with himself. Finally,

I asked what he was thinking about. "Oh, I'm just thinking about what's really important, that's all. My kids have a chance to have their mother back. I never had that chance. Can I stand in the way of *their* potential happiness just because *I* feel wronged—for the second time in my life?"

"You'll have to let go, then," I said. "And boy, if you do it will be one of the biggest rights anybody ever let go of. The question is this: What are you, in your heart, committed to: being right about how wronged you and the children were—or allowing and even encouraging them to have a positive relationship with their mother and maybe even a normal family life?"

"When you think about it like that, it seems obvious," Jerry said. "What kind of guy would I be if I stood in the way of their ultimate happiness, just because I was right and wanted to stand on principle? In the end, I'd never forgive myself."

"You won't have to, Jerry," I said, "but it sure would be good if you could forgive your wife. And then maybe your kids can forgive her, too. And that would create the best of all possible outcomes."

Jerry let go of his anger, he let go of being right, and he even let go of not wanting his children to love their mother as much as they loved him—and that was possibly the biggest letting-go of all.

Except for one: Jerry decided to let go of being right about how wrong his mother was to leave him all those years ago. In our conversations about her, we decided that it was possible that his mother did the only thing she could do, that she was incapable of acting differently. If we looked at it that way, there was no use in staying angry—at least not all these decades later. So Jerry forgave his mother. Not only did he forgive her, but he set out on a pilgrimage to find her. And he did. After a great deal of sleuthing, Jerry even found her phone number and called her. When she answered, he said, "Hello, Mom. This is Jerry. Your son. I love you."

Now Jerry's children have not only a mother but a grandmother as well.

Okay, it's your turn now. What "rights" from the past are you going to give up? And will you commit to catching yourself when the being-right monster rears its ugly head? Remember, just press PAUSE and ask yourself what you're really committed to. It's more fun to find fulfillment than it is to find fault. And you'll be amazed at the difference it will make in your life. People will smile when they see you coming. You'll probably start whistling. And heaven knows, you'll look better. I'm not kidding about the Botox thing.

Add the "rights" to your Mental Throw-Outs list, okay? Otherwise, I'll have to do *just a minute*. And you don't want that.

Steps for letting go of needing to be right about how wrong it is:

1. Ask yourself this: *Do I want to be right or do I want to be happy?*
2. Here's another question to ask: *What's more important to me: Making someone else wrong for the moment or having a great long-term or productive relationship?*
3. Let somebody else be right for a minute before you make your point. Say this: "You're right. I totally get where you're coming from." Then give your opinion. This will work miracles, I'm not kidding.
4. Make a list of at least five things you've been right about that you're throwing out.

Gail's Throw-Out Scorecard:

I will throw out saying, "Just a minute, that's not right . . ." whenever I'm annoyed with a person or a situation—until I've asked myself what I'm committed to: being right, or having a happy, positive long-term outcome.

Total: 1 thing
Running Total: 45 things

<u>Your Throw-Out Scorecard:</u>

_____

_____

_____

_____

_____

_____

Your Total:

Your Running Total:

Chapter 15

Letting Go of the Need to Have *Everyone* Like You

When I was a little girl about nine years old, living in Bay Village, Ohio, I came home from some-one's birthday party and burst into tears. "What's wrong?" my mother asked. "Suzy doesn't like me!" I wailed. "How do you know?" my mom asked. "Because everyone says so," I answered, like a typical nine-year-old. "Hmm," Mom said, "that's interesting." And then after a minute or two she added, "Darling, can you think of anything that everybody in the whole world likes?" I just looked at her, sniffling. "Because I can think of only one thing," she said, "and that's water. And that's because it has no taste. Do you want to be like water?" I thought for a minute. "I guess not," I said. "Good," my mother said, "I didn't think so." "Maybe I'll be like hot chocolate or Coca-Cola—or, I know, lemonade!" "Terrific," she said, "now you've got it."

What a great mom, you're thinking, right? And she was. The best. And I wish I could say I've always lived by her words, but I haven't. I can't tell you how often I've gotten caught up in the need to be everyone's everything, to be universally appealing, like type O blood. I mean what's not to like?

I don't think it's just me. I bet you're thinking right now about the times *you've* fallen into the I-need-everybody-to-like-me trap. I don't think I've met anyone who hasn't. But why? I mean, when you really think about it, who is loved—or even liked—by absolutely everyone? Look at some of the people who really stand out in our society: Donald Trump, Madonna, Cher, Tom Cruise, Oprah—and what about Rosie? Some people love 'em, some people hate 'em. And when you think about it, there have always been people like that. Gloria Steinem always stood apart. Looking farther back, so did Eleanor Roosevelt (not to mention her husband) and Winston Churchill. Most of these people are, or were, controversial. I doubt any of them would have lasted very long if they had worried about being universally liked. And although they were vastly different, they all had one thing in common. They knew this: *If enough people love you, the ones who don't, don't matter.*

But most of us are afraid to be controversial, or even who we really are. We're like lemonade with too much water in it and too few lemons. We dilute our flavor so we won't offend anyone. And in the process, we give away our power, the essence of who we are; the very thing that makes us unique and unforgettable.

But that's hardly surprising. We're pretty used to

tamping down what makes us different and pointing up what makes us the same as other people, aren't we? From the time we're little, our parents, our teachers, our bosses have all coached us not to get carried away but to conform, to fit in, to be well liked. And we spend a lot of effort and money in following their advice. We buy the right clothes, wear the right makeup, drive the right car, say the right things—all so that we can get the approval of as many people as possible.

Remember *Death of a Salesman,* the landmark play by Arthur Miller? The protagonist, Willy Loman, counsels his son Biff: "Be liked and you will never want." But ironically, at the end of the play it's Biff's friend Bernard—the nerdy guy Willy made fun of, the guy who is not "well liked"—who becomes not only successful and respected, but happy.

The truth is, the world belongs not to the one who fits in but to the one who stands out. In music, art, architecture, entertainment, politics, and *life,* it's the maverick, the one who gets carried away, who wins the day. Every time.

Okay, so if you and I intend to be unique—and maybe even unforgettable—we can't be everybody's everything. We have to *decide*—there's that word again—who we are at the core and what distinguishes us from the herd. So that means we have to *let go of* the old habit of getting upset if someone thinks we're a little too lemony or have a bit too much fizz for his or her taste.

And speaking of fizz, I know a brilliant, accomplished woman named Liz who found herself in a compromising spot not long ago—she had to decide who she was and who she wasn't. It was a tough decision because the stakes were high. She reported to the CEO of a small advertising agency, Mark—a man who had seemed to think highly of her as she'd made her way up the ladder from assistant account executive to vice president. But as Liz increased her visibility both inside and outside the company (the advertising trades included her frequently in their "who's news" columns), her boss's "liking" of her decreased. He liked her all right when she was struggling to make her way upward, but once she'd arrived, he didn't. A friend and colleague gave her this advice: "Liz, if you want to stick around here, you're going to have to lay low. Mark doesn't like all the attention you're getting. I don't know if he's jealous or just mean-spirited, but I think you'll have to change your act if you don't want to make him mad—and take the consequences." Liz was stunned. She'd thought, as most of us do, that if she worked hard and got good results, everything else would fall into place. Recently, she'd felt she'd really hit her groove. It just never had occurred to her that she could be *too* good or *too* strong for anyone's liking.

When Liz and I met, she was almost at the end of her rope. Every morning, she got up and wondered if she were going to inadvertently do something, even something good, that might annoy her boss. "What if I get fired?" she asked me. "You know, that's not outside the realm of possibility. Mark could concoct all sorts of reasons why I'm not performing up to speed. I've seen him do it with other people, now that I think of it."

Liz was forty, had been with the company twelve years, and had stock options, a bonus, and other perks that made for a pretty nice life. She was also the major bread-winner for her family. Getting fired was definitely a scary thought.

"What about quitting?" I asked.

"Are you kidding?" Liz said, shocked.

"Actually, I'm not," I said quietly. "Here's the thing, You've got two choices: You can stick around here and wait for Mark to feel more secure and less intimidated by you, which could take another twelve years or so, and all the while you can lay low, play small, and try not to be too good. Or you can blow this joint and get on with your life."

"Gail, I really need this job."

"I know," I replied, "but there are other jobs in other companies with other stock options and other bonuses and, best of all, other bosses, who would be thrilled to have someone with your energy and élan. Think about it for a minute."

I reminded her of how miserable she was going to work every day, of how, incredible as it seemed, she had actually outpaced, outclassed, and outgrown her small-minded boss. It took her a while to believe me. She'd just never thought of herself as intimidating. Most of us don't. "But up until now, I had a good time here," Liz said. "I just don't get what went wrong."

"Nothing went wrong," I said. "It's just time to move on. And ironically, *it's time to be more yourself, not less.* Let's take an inventory of who you really are."

Liz and I made a list of the things she'd done so far in her career that made her feel the proudest—and I'd like you to do the same. Because once Liz started thinking about it, she was surprised by how much she'd accomplished—and you will be, too. Like most of us, she'd never really focused on how good she already was; she was always too busy just trying to get up for the next challenge. She remembered having stood in at the last minute, about a year earlier, for a very senior person who was ill, and having made a critical presentation to the firm's biggest client. She had been completely terrified but she'd pulled it off, not perfectly but impressively, and with grace and humor. The client team had applauded when she'd finished. Liz was grinning as she told me the story.

Next, we made a list of the qualities she liked best about herself. (You do it, too. It's easy.) Without a moment's hesitation, she put down "funny." Then she added "sensitive," "motivating," and "a good listener."

And then I invited Liz to do one of my favorite exercises. (You remember it from chapter 8, "Clarifying Your

Brand.") "Complete this sentence," I said, *"I'm Liz and I'm the one who . . ."* "Oh boy, I've got to think about that," she replied. "No, don't make it hard," I said. "What do you want to be known for, what would make you the proudest? When you say *I'm the one who,* you're making a promise. What's your promise?"

"Okay," Liz said, "here goes." She stood up, put her shoulders back, smiled, and said, *"I'm Liz. I'm the one who gets it done.* And," she added, "I make doing it fun."

How did you complete that sentence? Say it out loud and listen to how good it sounds.

Now here was where the rubber met the road. I asked Liz what she was going to throw out in order to live up to her promise.

Here's what she said: "I'm going to throw out thinking that if somebody doesn't like me, it's my fault. I'm going to let go of thinking that I have to please everyone all the time—or else I'm not good enough. And I'm going to let go of being afraid to stand out in a crowd. How's that?"

"Perfect," I said.

Well, I don't have to tell you how it all turned out. Liz resigned. You know that old adage, don't leave a job until you have another one? Well, don't you believe it. At least not *all* the time. Of course, there are times when, dictated by financial or family constraints, we have to nail the new job before we can leave the old one. But there are also times when we have to let go of a debilitating past in order to hasten the appearance of an exciting future. Liz was a new person from the moment she told Mark she was moving on. She looked different; she sounded different. She was exactly what she needed to be: She was unabashedly herself. She was "back."

Six weeks later, Liz landed a new job at a hot new agency, renowned for its superb client relations. "We love your attitude," her new boss told her when he offered her the job, "you've got the kind of spirit we need around here. Congratulations!" Less than six months after she joined the new firm, she brought in her old firm's biggest client—the one she'd made that killer presentation to.

Speaking of "killer presentations," good as Liz's was, there was probably someone in the audience who didn't think it was all that impressive. There always is. And that's true for all of us. **Because no matter how terrific we are, not everybody will buy our act. It's just not possible. And it doesn't matter. So let's throw out thinking we're not good if one person thinks we're mediocre. Okay? That's a deal.**

My father, the most motivating person I've ever known, said whenever I felt fainthearted about standing out, standing tall, or standing apart: "Stand for something or you'll fall for anything." Liz almost fell for playing small, for being less than she was, for diluting her uniqueness so she wouldn't offend or intimidate. Don't do it. Remember who you are. Remember what makes you not water—or even hot chocolate or Coca-Cola—but the most delicious glass of lemonade anyone ever tasted. Review your own list of unique qualities every day without fail. Embrace yourself as you embrace these qualities. Walk into every room demonstrating your fabulous, one-of-a-kind self. And when the old fear pops up—that fear of not pleasing—throw it out and think about Cher or Madonna, or good ol' Rosie, and remember, you're the one who . . .

The world is longing for you to step forward in all your lemony goodness, not in some watered-down version. And not all, but enough people will welcome you with open arms. Hey, if enough people love ya, the ones who don't, don't matter.

Steps for letting go of needing everyone to like you:

1. Make a list of all the qualities you like best about yourself—everything from your humor to your passion for persuasion; whatever makes you feel unique. Ask people to whom you're close to add to the list.

2. Commit to not playing small just because someone else is intimidated by how big you could be. Whenever possible, eliminate those people from your life.

3. Complete this sentence without fail: *I'm _____, and I'm the one who . . .* This is your promise. Keep it.

4. Make a list of the things you're afraid people won't like about you. Throw every one of those fears out. Because if enough people love ya, the ones who don't, don't matter.

Gail's Throw-Out Scorecard:

I will throw out thinking that absolutely everyone has to love what I say, what I write, or what I do.

Total: 1 thing
Running Total: 46 things

Your Throw-Out Scorecard:

_____

_____

_____

_____

_____

_____

Your Total:
Your Running Total:

Chapter 16

Letting Go of Thinking the Worst

Boy, if you can throw this one out, you can really be happy. I'm serious. Negative interpretations get all over us like that gluey stuff that some insects spew out of their mouths to trap and kill other bugs. I think the Venus flytrap has something similar on its leaves that it uses to trap its prey. Actually, we're all like the lovely Venus flytrap, aren't we? Something happens, somebody says something, and *snap!* We turn whatever it is into something bad, stick it in our psyches, and chew on it. And unlike Miss Venus F., we don't thrive on it, we make ourselves sick over it.

A few years ago, I had just given a speech for a large corporation and was heading for the elevators when the head of human resources accosted me. "Hey, Gail," she said, "do you remember when we were having lunch earlier and you were looking at me really hard?" "Uh, yeah," I said, "sort of." "Well, I know you were thinking something was wrong with my makeup," she continued, looking worried. "I mean you used to work at a cosmetics company and everything—so tell me, what should I be doing differently?"

"Are you kidding?" I said. "Boy, have you got that wrong. I was looking at you so hard because I was listening to you so hard. I wanted to catch every word you said."

"Are you sure?" she asked, looking at me with narrowed eyes. "I sure am," I said. "You look terrific. Honest."

I was finally able to convince her before I got into the elevator that her makeup was fine, but it wasn't easy. She was positive she was right. And the fact was, I *was* looking at her hard. And her automatic interpretation was that something was wrong—in this case, with her makeup. We do this all the time, right? Here's what happens: Something happens or someone says something—a fact—and in a heartbeat, we make it mean something; an interpretation. And then bingo! The fact and the interpretation get mooshed together and that becomes the "truth"; worse, it becomes our reality.

When I started writing this book, I sent several chapters to my editor, Karen Murgolo, and asked her to just give them a quick read. When I'd done that before, she'd always gotten back to me in less than two days with a point of view. This time, I hadn't head from her for a week and a half. "I haven't heard from Karen," I told Jim. "So?" he said. "She's probably busy with other stuff." "No, she always gets right back to me," I told him. "There must be something wrong; I was taking some chances with those chapters, she probably doesn't like them. Now I'm going to have to rewrite them and I'm already behind schedule." Jim rolled his eyes. "Aren't you getting a little worked up for nothing? She liked the last ones you sent, why wouldn't she like these? Why don't you just be optimistic until you hear otherwise?"

Now, that was really good advice when you think about it. But I was pressured with a lot of work and my energy was really low. And like with most of us, low energy breeds worry and insecurity. So I added the very "real" possibility of Karen not liking my chapters to my list of other things I was worried about. Not surprisingly, I only slept a few hours that night. Most of my time in bed was spent flailing about, sighing and thinking of all the stuff that could go wrong. It didn't matter that there were no real facts to support my concerns. My interpretations took over. And all my interpretations—for just about anything that had happened during the previous week—were negative. I hadn't heard back from a financial institution about whether or not they were sending me to Dubai to give an important speech to some of their most valued people in the Asia Pacific Rim. Which probably meant they'd chosen someone else, right? And I hadn't gotten word from David Molko, a producer for a television network who'd gotten approval for producing a special piece on women and heart disease featuring the story of my own "heart caper." So he probably didn't get the bucks, right? The list went on and on. One night really wasn't long enough to toss and turn over this stuff. It could take a week.

Actually, it did. The bags under my eyes couldn't be erased with the best undereye concealer, or ice packs, tea bags, or, as it turned out, even good ol' Botox. "You just need to lighten up," said Alan Matarasso, a good friend and plastic surgeon. "Sounds like you're worrying about stuff you shouldn't be worrying about. Stop that, and the rest will take care of itself." Again, wise words from a wise man. But easier said than done, don't you think? Especially when all these negative interpretations added up to one thing: not good enough. Those are the three words that summarize many of our middle-of-the-night tossings.

So did I lighten up? No. Not until I heard from Karen that she was sorry it had taken so long to read my chapters, but she'd been swamped by another project and they looked fine; not until I'd heard from the financial institution that they'd had an emergency to deal with but that they were, indeed, sending me to Dubai; and not until David called and said they'd gotten the budget and they were going forward with the piece. So that all added up to about two weeks of my making myself really unhappy—needlessly.

And what was worse, I weakened my mental immune system by being so irrationally worried, to the point that the slightest little thing that didn't work out, or where I could possibly blame myself for messing up, was proof that those three awful words were right: *not good enough*. Can you believe it? Is that any way to live? Does any of this seem even faintly familiar to you? And here's the thing: None of my interpretations of what happened, or hadn't happened, was accurate. I'd made up a lot of negative stuff out of fear that life just wouldn't work out the way I wanted it to at this moment, or that somehow I wouldn't measure up. And I'd hung on to these negative interpretations at exactly the moment when I should have thrown them out.

Look, our lives are awash in interpretations. Wars are fought over interpretations. Elections are won or lost over interpretations. The stock market moves up or down based not on facts but the interpretations of those facts. It's true, Karen didn't call me back for a while. That's a fact. It was also a fact that I didn't hear back from the producer or the corporate executive from the financial institution. But it wasn't the facts that kept me from sleeping; it was the interpretations.

Look back into your life; look back to yesterday or this morning. Something happened, somebody said something; what did you make it mean? Maybe someone didn't answer your e-mail about an idea you wanted to recommend, or return your call about your request for information about a new position you're interested in. Or maybe somebody just looked at you the wrong way in a meeting, or on the street, or in an elevator. What did you make it mean? Not something good, I bet. And then the rest of the day you lived with that negative thought floating around in your brain, and zap, there goes a power drain. And before you know it, you're stumbling along the street with your head down or walking into a room expecting something else to go wrong. And the funny thing is, nothing's gone wrong at all. You just made it all up.

When I was on *The Oprah Winfrey Show* with my book called *In My Wildest Dreams,* I came close to ruining one of the best opportunities a girl could have by slapping a negative interpretation on something that happened. Oprah's producer had told me that before we started taping my show (I was lucky enough to be the solo guest), they were going to tape some openings and closings for other shows. "You wait in the green room," she said. "It won't take us very long. And then we'll get your show on the road, okay? And Gail," she added, "I'm going to want a lot of energy from you, kiddo, okay? A lot. This whole show is about energy, you know what I mean?"

"I do," I said, "but shouldn't we talk some more about exactly what we're going to do? You know, once we start taping?"

"Kiddo," she said, "it's simple. When we're done with the other stuff, I'll come and get you, and I'll bring Oprah so you can have a chance to chat for a few minutes, and then we'll go out onto the set. There will be two big yellow chairs. Oprah will sit in one and you'll sit in the other. And you guys will start talking and it'll take off from there. But Gail," she said, "I really do need a lot of energy, okay? I'll see you after a while."

I sat in the green room all by myself—for an hour and

a half. Do you know what can happen in an hour and a half? I'll tell you: You pretty much forget everything you ever knew. "I wish I'd brought my book with me," I said out loud to no one at all. "Then maybe I could remember something I wrote. I mean, if I could even just read the introduction, it might get me kick-started or something . . ."

At that point the producer came in and said, "We're running a little late, kiddo, so you won't have a chance to chat with Oprah, but let's go get 'em, okay? Lots of energy, got it? Badda bing."

So we walked out onto the set. Yes, there were two big, yellow chairs there and Oprah was sitting in one. The other was empty. I walked up to Oprah, put out my hand, and said, "Hi, I'm Gail." "How're you doing?" she said. "Good," I said. "Good," she said. And that was it. She didn't ask me to sit down, so I didn't. I just stood there. She thought for a minute and then turned to the show's director and said these three words, words that are now needlepointed onto a pillow in my office, words that I'll never forget: "Get the bench."

Get the bench? I thought. What does that mean? Oh, I know, I bet that's code for "get the hook." Oprah's a very smart woman, and she knows when she's run into somebody who's forgotten everything she ever knew, who has no energy, no badda bing, nothing. Two guys came out and quickly removed the two chairs and replaced them with a big yellow bench.

Oprah said, "Okay, Gail, you sit on the bench. I'm

going out into the audience." And she did. And there I was sitting alone on a bench in front of potentially millions of people, having forgotten just about everything I ever knew. I looked out into the audience and saw my daughter Kate. She raised her eyebrows. I answered her by raising mine. And then I thought, *What am I doing here, anyway? What ever made me think I was good enough to be on* Oprah? I wanted to go home. Or at least, lie down.

The *fact* was, Oprah had said, "Get the bench," and there I was sitting on it—alone. What did it mean? Well, the first *interpretation* I came up with was easy: *Oprah doesn't like me,* I thought. *It's as simple as that. The woman doesn't even want to sit next to me.* The next interpretation that occurred to me was, *That's not very nice, putting a woman you don't even know on a bench by herself.* That wasn't going to help, either. So what was I to do? (See? For a minute, I wanted to be *right* about Oprah being *wrong.* That never works.)

So here's what I did and here's what you have to do, too: When something happens, when somebody says something, before we slap a negative interpretation on it, we've got to wait one second and ask this question: *What am I committed to?* And then we've got to *throw out the negative interpretation* and make up an interpretation that will help us accomplish the thing we're out for.

The good news is that I actually knew what I was committed to: I wanted to ensure that every single person in Oprah's audience would leave with a new sense of what was possible in her life. *Okay, "kiddo,"* I said, *if that's what you're out for, what the heck are you going to make "get the bench" mean?* And I came up with this: "Oprah trusts me." And that interpretation changed everything. *If Oprah trusts me,* I thought, *who am I not to trust myself?* So I just started talking. (You know how sometimes you just have to start, even when you don't know exactly where it will lead?) And eventually, I even got up off the bench and moved into the audience. And Oprah joined me. And I think—actually I know—that together we changed some lives that day.

A few days later, the producer called me in New York and said, "Hey, Gail, just wanted you to know—we're editing the show and it's looking good. I think you'll be pleased."

"Gee, that's great," I said. "But I've been wondering. You know when Oprah said, 'Get the bench'?"

"Yeah, that was big," the producer said.

"Oh, yeah, I knew that," I lied, "but I was just wondering, like, you know, what did that mean?"

"Oh, that just means that Oprah's telling you to go ahead and take the show," she said.

"Of course. I knew that, too," I said, fumbling. "I mean, I was just checking. Hey, you were terrific to call."

One can only imagine what would have happened if I'd hung on to one of those negative interpretations . . .

"Wait a darned minute, Gail," you're saying. "What if you'd been right about your editor not liking the chapters, or the corporation not choosing you to speak, or the producer not caring enough about the segment to find the money for it, or Oprah actually not liking you? What if it turned out you *weren't* good enough?"

Okay, what if the worst *had* happened? And you know what, sometimes, it does. We don't always get our heart's desire, our act bombs, and the trip to Dubai goes to someone else. But you know what? The bad stuff happens so much less frequently than we think it will! Most of the time things work out okay. And sometimes they work out gangbusters.

So listen, we've got to cut this out. We've got to decide here and now, once and for all, that we're going to *let go* of slapping negative interpretations on the stuff that happens or the things that are said in any given day. We're going to press PAUSE for just one second and we're going to ask ourselves this one question: *What am I out for, anyway?* What do I want to make happen? Is it a promotion, a new job, a new boyfriend, approval for a big new project, or just a happy ending to a tough day? **Then no matter what happens, assign a positive interpretation to the current situation. In the end, you'll have a much better chance of getting what you truly want, no matter how big or small it is.**

And remember what Albert Einstein said: "Ultimately, there are no facts." See? It's pretty much all interpretation. It's pretty much all made up. So if it's all made up, then *you* make it up. Make up interpretations that propel you forward toward the life of your dreams, not the ones that drag you back into a past you're supposed to be done with. This is your life, you know. Not some movie you're watching. You get to decide how it all turns out. You get to make it up. *So make it up good.*

Steps for clearing the clutter of negative interpretations:

1. Make a list of some of the major things that have occurred in your life during the last year or so.

2. How did you interpret these events? Were your interpretations correct? Or were there instances where you never even found out what the "correct" interpretations were?

3. Ask yourself how needlessly unhappy you made yourself, having assumed a negative interpretation. Ask yourself how much energy you gave up putting yourself down.

4. Make another list of what you consider the reality of your life to be right now—what's likely to happen with your relationships, your career, your health, your financial situation. Ask yourself what parts of these so-called realities are actual fact—and which you've made up, given your fears, your resignation, or some old habit of saying to yourself, "It's better to assume the worst; then when things work out okay, you can be pleasantly surprised." Boy, what a crummy way to live each day. Don't do it. Let it go.

Gail's Throw-Out Scorecard:

I will throw out assuming that "no news is bad news."

Total: 1 thing
Running Total: 47 things

Your Throw-Out Scorecard:

_____

_____

_____

_____

_____

_____

Your Total:
Your Running Total:

Chapter 17

Letting Go of Waiting for the Right Moment

Waiting is a national pastime. We wait for the mood to strike us, we wait for the weather to change, we wait for someone to strike up the band and give us our cue to start singing. Some of us are waiting for them to get it about us. You know, about how good we are. They should recognize us and promote us and celebrate us. They should discover us. But that's not how it works. Here's how it works: People don't get it about us until we get it about ourselves. Until we step out of the stands and onto the field—even before we're invited.

Speaking of national pastimes and stepping onto the field, here's a story you'll get a kick out of . . .

When I was about twenty-four, I had one of the all-time best jobs in the world, especially for a girl. I was manager of special promotions for the New York Yankees. Yup, the only woman in Major League Baseball with what they called a front-office job. Well, I knew a little bit about baseball and less about promotions—but I applied myself rigorously and had an awful lot of fun.

I went to every single home game and figured that I probably ate more hot dogs than any other woman in America. One day when I was on the phone, one of the players, a real star (we'll call him Joe), plopped himself down in a chair in my small office and started eating a giant pastrami sandwich. He looked morose. When I got off the phone, I said, "Joe, what's the matter?" With his mouth full and mustard dribbling down his chin (Joe was known for his hitting, not his table manners), he said, "I'm in a slump. I gotta wait for it to be over." It was true that Joe had struck out the last three times at bat, so as far as he and the sportswriters were concerned, that was a "slump." I thought about it for a minute. I sure didn't want Joe to leave my office the same way he'd arrived, so I tried to think of something motivational to say.

"I don't know, Joe, about the slump thing—and why you have to wait for it to be over. Why can't you just decide, like now, that it's over?" "That's baseball," Joe said, "you don't understand." "I know I don't," I said, "but who makes this stuff up and why should we buy into it? The idea of waiting for a stupid slump to be over doesn't even make any sense."

Joe looked at me like I was a complete idiot and just a girl who didn't get it about baseball. (He actually wasn't all that far off.) But I was young and on a roll so I plunged on. "Look," I said, "three strikeouts equals three strikeouts, *not four*. Let's declare that the slump is over as of this moment. Done. It's done, Joe. Just get up there and hit the darned ball, will you? Don't hold back; don't wait. It's what you're here for, right? And nobody does it better." Joe kept chewing. After a minute or two, he stood up, grunted, and walked out. Naturally, he left the remains of his sandwich, pickles, and wadded-up napkins on my desk. But that didn't matter. What mattered was that he walked up to the plate a couple of hours later and hit a double. The next batter brought him home. When he was rounding third, he glanced up into the stands where I always sat, and touched his hat. That slump was over.

We are all much more powerful than we think. Much better equipped than we give ourselves credit for—to control our destinies and live, not the life we're resigned to, but the life we aspire to. **Not later. Now. And now is the time for us to let go of thinking that we're just not ready; that we have to perfect our act; that we have to wait.**

I know a woman named Jenny who should be ready to move forward in her career. All the signs point to this being the right time to take the step: She's recognized as an expert in her field, her company is open to promoting her, and, most importantly, she's lost enthusiasm for her current job.

"C'mon, Jenny, let's go for it," I said, somewhat impatiently. We'd been having the conversation about moving forward for weeks. "I know, I know, Gail, I should make my move pretty soon. But you know, I'm just waiting for my son to get a little older."

"Wait, how old is he now?" I asked.

"Well, he'll be thirty on his next birthday, but I just want to be sure . . ." She trailed off.

Look, many of us are waiting. We're waiting for the signal, or for the invitation, or to be discovered, or for the planets to be aligned before we take that step to change our lives or our world. (I'm not kidding. A friend of mine won't move forward with her life at all if Mercury is in retrograde. You don't do that, do you?) We put our power and our futures on hold and wait for the right moment to present itself. And while we're waiting, our lives, our opportunities, our big moments, float on by. As I've learned, sometimes the hard way, moments don't present themselves, you've got to go out and grab hold of them. And that takes courage.

A word about courage: Recently, a newly retired executive and I were talking about how important it was to make the *decision* to act. After a long silence, he looked up and said, "Okay, Gail, I've decided what I'm going to do. I'm going to write a book."

"That's great!" I said, "You've got a lot to say. When are you going to write it?" "Well," he answered, "I guess I just have to wait for the courage."

"Never wait for the courage," I said. "You could wait a lifetime."

It's true: No one is going to knock on your door one

fine day with a beautifully gift-wrapped box and say, "Here's your courage. Where do you want me to put it?" Here's the thing about courage: It isn't given. Which is good because it can't be taken away.

Courage comes with action. The minute you step forward, the minute you declare your decision, the minute you say, "This is how it's going to go," courage comes. It floods through you and energizes every single fiber of your being. You don't have to wait for it. It'll be there.

Here's a poignant story about a lovely woman who waited for her courage . . . for nineteen years.

Her name's Lue Ann Eldar and she's currently very successful and very much involved with charitable organizations in the New York area. She knows how good she is, how worthy she is of being listened to, of leading, of taking hold of her life—now. But back in 1978 when she was twenty-three, Lue Ann had a passion for classical music and a huge admiration for one of the great opera impresarios, Sir Rudolf Bing. For years, Sir Rudolf had been general manager of the Metropolitan Opera. So Lue Ann wrote to ask if he would agree to meet with her and consider taking her on as an intern.

About a week later, she received a letter back from Sir Rudolf's office. She looked at the envelope long and hard, turned it over and over, but didn't open it. In fact, she didn't open it that week or that month or even that year. She kept it unopened in a box with some "forget-table" keepsakes, taking it out now and then but never even breaking the seal on the envelope—unbelievably, for nineteen years. Now, that's a long wait.

"Lue Ann," I said, "I can't believe it! Why in the world . . ." "Because," she said, "I didn't think I was good enough. I only saw my flaws and failures. And, frankly, I just didn't want to know that he had rejected me. I didn't want to read what I was sure would be his *Thanks but no thanks* response. I thought I'd better just wait." How many of us have done something similar, maybe not as dramatic, but similar? How many of us, to one degree or another, have simply taken ourselves out of the game so that we couldn't lose—and lost anyway. Here's what happened to Lue Ann.

In 1997, Sir Rudolf died. It was only then, only when she'd read his obituary in the *New York Times,* that Lue Ann found the courage to retrieve the letter from its box, open it, and read these words from the impresario himself: "I'd be delighted to meet with you," he wrote. "You sound like a very accomplished and talented young woman. Please call my office to set up an appointment. I look forward to hearing from you."

Lue Ann was stunned. She was both thrilled and appalled. Thrilled that Sir Rudolf had found her worthy enough to meet with him all those years ago; appalled that she had waited for the right moment and in the process, had completely blown the opportunity.

As you know by now, I believe that most things work out the way they're supposed to and that one of the best things we can do for ourselves is to let go of the so-called mistakes and regrets of the past. And Lue Ann, by the time she told me this story, had already done that. "It happened," she said. "My fear of rejection, my decision to wait until I felt more worthy, was nothing short of dumb. I learned from it. And that lesson has served me brilliantly for decades." Yes, it has. Today Lue Ann is one of the bravest, most self-confident people I know. And believe me, she doesn't wait. She steps into her power every day. She's propelled forward by her vision of making a positive difference in the world and boy, is she doing it. I just wish Sir Rudolf were here to give her a standing ovation.

So the waiting thing has got to go on our list of Mental Throwaways. Whenever you hear yourself say, "Maybe I'd better wait for . . ."—hold it right there. You don't have time to wait. Remember? This is the only life you have—at least the only one you know of for sure. And while you're waiting around for the right moment before you decide to try for that corner office job, or try for *Dancing With the Stars* (hey, why not?), or go meet that guy from eHarmony (and you've struck out three times before) remember this: The past can't dictate the future. You're the cause and the effect. You get to decide how it's going to go. Why not make it good? And make it *now*.

Steps for letting go of waiting for the right moment to step forward:

1. Don't disqualify yourself from the race before it even begins. You're here to compete, not to sit on the sidelines.

2. Make a list of your wins: the times you made the catch, made the call, or made the day—yours or someone else's. Revel in those wins every time you face a new challenge.

3. Abandon the list of your losses. To embrace your power, you have let go of your fear of losing or being rejected. Remember: Courage comes with action.

4. Just as you're about to step forward and that old voice cries out, "Wait!"—don't listen. Speak up anyway. Present your plan, declare your passion, walk up to the plate anyway. And when the envelope arrives, open it.

Gail's Throw-Out Scorecard:

I will throw out thinking that if I'm really good, they'll discover me—and walk out onto the field with all my flags flying.

Total: 1 thing
Running Total: 48 things

Your Throw-Out Scorecard:

_____

Your Total:
Your Running Total:

Chapter 18

Letting Go of Needing to Feel Secure

We all have those moments when we don't know where we're headed—or even who we are. We frequently find ourselves thrashing about in the in-between parts of our lives: in between jobs, in between relationships, in between an old idea of ourselves and a new one. And it's bloody uncomfortable, isn't it? I mean, security was always the Holy Grail. You remember: There was national security and personal security, right? That's when we knew that, no matter what, we'd be safe. Remember Social Security? (Actually, maybe it's better not to remember that right now.) And how about job security? Financial security? There was this idea that if you worked and saved and kept a lid on your wildest dreams, not to mention your expenses, you'd be fine. You'd go straight up the ladder from job to job in the same company and then *bingo:* Florida! And the house right smack on the golf course. Well, all those securities are, if not totally defunct, more than a little iffy these days.

A few years ago, I was a guest speaker at a class reunion

at Princeton University. At one point, I asked each of the alumni to finish the sentence, *Twenty-five years ago, I never would have thought that I...* One attractive gal stood up and said, "Twenty-five years ago I never would have thought that I'd be standing here, a Princeton graduate—with honors, mind you—saying, 'I have no idea where I'm going or what my career and my life should be about for the next twenty-five years.'"

Two-thirds of the room stood and applauded her honesty and nodded in commiseration. I went up to her later and introduced myself. Her name was Claire. She was recently divorced, with two almost grown children, and had just been downsized from an investment banking firm. She couldn't believe that her life had turned out like this. "I feel so insecure," she said.

"It hasn't turned out," I replied. "This is just an inconvenient moment in a long and, hopefully, colorful life. And anyway, it could be good."

"Are you kidding?" said Claire. "I don't know where I'm headed. I can't see the future. I'm not even sure I know who I am right now."

"That's why it's good," I said.

Look, I know it's hard to swallow at first—it was for Claire, and it has been for me—but I believe with my whole heart that it's okay *not to know*. Insecurity—not knowing what the future holds for us—can be good, not bad. When you think about it, we weren't meant to live tidy, predictable lives with everything neatly laid out in front of us, like all our clothes for the next week. You know, our skirts, shirts, shoes, earrings, belts, purses, all of it—folded up and labeled like the inevitable parade dress of an automaton whose only wish is to fulfill its already prescribed destiny.

No, I think being comfortable, which Merriam-Webster's defines as "enjoying contentment and security . . . free from vexation or doubt," actually stunts growth. I'm not kidding. If we're absolutely comfortable and totally secure, if we long for nothing, worry about nothing, aspire only to more of the same, where is the impetus to grow, to change, to invent, to *reinvent.* Where in the world is Darwin in that equation? Nowhere. And Darwin, my friend, was right. He said, "It's not the strongest of the species that survives, or even the smartest. It's the one who can adapt to change."

Guess what? We're the "species." We're fabulous, living, breathing organisms without any limits to where our evolution can take us. We're always, thank goodness, on our way; never there. And just for the record, it's supposed to be an adventure. An adventure, by its very nature, is unpredictable; the outcome is unknown. Otherwise, it wouldn't be an adventure. And Thomas à Becket was right. *It isn't* written until we write it.

The fact is, we can't grow if we always stay in our comfort zones. But most of us don't move out into the unknown, into the land of adventure, willingly. That's why it's good when we're pushed out. Claire would still be in her old firm, which she described to me as "deadly and debilitating," and she might still be married to the same guy, whom she described as "small-minded and self-absorbed," if the universe hadn't had the good sense to pull the rug out from under her and set her in motion. Jolts like that are hard to take—insecurity is not what we were brought up to value or expect—yet they can come along at any moment. **And our choices are to hunker down, wrap ourselves in what we already know, and wait for things to go back to the way they were (good luck with that one), or step into the unknown with all flags flying—and grow, adapt, and flourish—like the strong, smart members of the species we are.** It doesn't have to be that hard. It can even be fun. But first we have to let go of that need to feel secure all the time.

Initially, though, Claire was so stuck in the *I'm smart so I should be in complete control of my destiny* paradigm that she needed some warm-up exercises just to get her to consider letting go of the handrails and stepping into the unknown. So here's Claire's warm-up list for letting go of needing to be secure. It worked for her. I think it will for you, too.

- Try new, exotic foods. Every week or two, go to a different restaurant that serves ethnic food or uses exotic ingredients that are foreign to you. Catch yourself when you're about to say, "But I don't like curry!" Try it anyway. Claire fell in love with Thai food and began using lemongrass in her own cooking.

- Listen to new music. Buy some CDs or download music you've never heard (or liked) before—maybe the music your kids listen to?—from Gregorian chants to salsa to rap. Claire took a class in African drumming with her daughter. At first she felt awkward, but her daughter encouraged her. They had a ball.

- Try a new sport. The idea is not to win the triathlon but to put yourself out there, to feel the discomfort of learning something new—and to do it anyway. Claire bought a bike and joined a group of cyclists in her neighborhood (people she'd never met before), and they now bike together every Saturday morning.

- Develop a student mentality. Your objective is to learn. See yourself going from coveting security to embracing insecurity and thriving on adventure. Now you're cookin'.

A friend said to Claire shortly after she was fired, "You should start your own company." Her response was, "You've got to be joking. I'm so not an entrepreneur." Today she has her own business, specializing in providing investment services and financial counseling to women in transition, and says she finds it "hugely rewarding." She bikes to her office. Oh, and she's dating a man she met at the Thai take-out place. She describes him as "really funny, an absolute delight." And, she says, he gets a huge kick out of her drumming.

Let go of needing to be secure, my friend. It's no fun. And as my dad would say, there's no percentage in it.

Steps for letting go of the need to be secure:

1. Let go of needing to know how it's all going to turn out. In the novel of your life, there's no skipping to the last page. There is no last page.

2. Let go of needing guarantees that your lives will evolve according to the plan you devised decades ago. Given half a chance, your life will evolve into something better than anything you could have imagined—even in your wildest dreams.

3. Let go of your conviction that if you can't imagine it, it can't happen. Most of the greatest possibilities in our lives are not currently on our radar screens. Now, that's exciting.

4. Make a list of your insecurities. Throw out at least 75 percent of them now. That'll make a nice addition to the total number of things you've thrown out, won't it?

Gail's Throw-Out Scorecard:

I will throw out fearing that if I can't see how it's all going to turn out, it's not going to turn out well.

Total: 1 thing
Running Total: 49 things

Your Throw-Out Scorecard:

_____

_____

_____

_____

_____

_____

Your Total:
Your Running Total:

Chapter 19

Letting Go of Thinking That You Have to Do Everything Yourself

The thing is, Gail," a friend of mine named Anne said a few years ago, "you've got to let go of thinking that you're alone; that you have to do everything yourself. It makes me tired watching you."

I was shocked. I had no idea I gave off that vibe. "C'mon, I don't do that, that's ridiculous," I replied.

"Think about it," she said. "There are all sorts of people who can help you, but not if you don't let them, or if they think that you don't need them. It's like you're turning away all these wonderful angels who are there for you. If you'd only notice them." Pretty profound, right?

Well, I thought about what Anne said off and on—mainly off—for the next couple of years. I was too busy trying to do everything myself to think about angels. And she and I lost track of each other, which was too bad because I could've used her insightful proddings. But then something happened that brought her words straight home—and now I try to live by them . . .

Two years ago, as I was pulling up to a departure gate

at O'Hare Airport in Chicago, I realized that I had all my bags on the right side of the cab and that it would be hard for me to climb over all my stuff to get out. "I'll just get out on the left and go around to get my bags from the right," I told the driver. I thought I heard him make a grunting noise to show he'd heard me, but looking back, I'm not so sure. I got out, closed the door, and at that exact moment the driver took off with all my stuff: my good "speech suit," all my makeup, my pricey skin care products, my favorite shoes, and a bag with all my work documents in it, including my laptop, BlackBerry—and yes, you won't believe it, my purse. My purse with my wallet, credit cards, passport, and a pair of diamond stud earrings tucked into the side pocket. It was like my life was in that cab.

I ran after him screaming, "Stop, come back! Hey! Come back!" Cars were honking and drivers were yelling at me to get out of the way. With tears starting to run down my face, I shouted at the curbside check-in guy, "My cab drove off with all my stuff!" He asked me what kind of cab it was. "I don't know," I said, "it was white with some black on it." He rolled his eyes and asked me what the number of the cab was. "I have no idea," I cried. "Well, then I can't help you. Do you have any idea how many cabdrivers and cab companies there are in Chicago? I'm afraid you're out of luck."

I can't be out of luck, I thought. *There's got to be somebody who can help me. Where are all those angels Anne talked about? Angels, my foot, here I am alone in this blasted airport without even . . .*

"The number on the cab was 047," a quiet voice said. I turned and found an attractive man about my age (whatever that is) looking at me a bit sternly. "Hey," he scolded, "that wasn't too smart running out into the traffic like that, you could've been killed. I saw the whole thing." "I know, I know," I said, "but he's got all my stuff, all my . . ." "Never mind," the man (whose name turned out to be Dan Blodgett) said. "We'll get him back here, I promise." Dan got on his cell phone and started calling all the cab companies on the list given him by the curbside check-in guy. He left messages at over a dozen firms. In between calls, he spoke quietly and reassuringly to me, and I actually started believing I just might get my stuff back. I mean, it would be a miracle, but Dan wasn't a bit worried and I took my cue from him. About half an hour later, his cell phone rang. I held my breath and willed that there would be good news. Dan listened for about thirty seconds, winked at me, and said, "Okay, so he's on his way back to the airport, right? And he's got all Ms. Blanke's luggage with him? Great. We'll be waiting right here." Dan never left my side until Cab 047 pulled up about half an hour later. And sure enough, all my stuff was right there in the backseat.

"You're an angel, Dan Blodgett," I told him. "And I'll never forget you." Dan smiled one more time and then disappeared into the crowd.

I can't be the only one, I thought on the plane ride back to New York. *I can't be the only one who thinks she has to handle everything*

by herself; that she's totally on her own. And I can't be the only one who was
surprised to find out she was wrong.

So I asked a few of my friends and colleagues if they'd ever experienced the appearance of "angels" in their lives. And boy, did the floodgates open. It turns out just about everyone I talk to has had one kind of experience or another where someone appeared in their lives "out of the blue" and saved the day, or even their lives, or just made them feel like the world, with all its flaws and failings, was a pretty good place after all. I bet you've got some stories of your own. Now would be a good time to remember them.

Meanwhile, here's a true story from my friend Laurel Bernstein to get you thinking: She was driving through a terrible surprise blizzard, trying to get home to her teenage son, when the visibility dropped to about two feet. Laurel knew the roads pretty well, so she kept going, but only at the rate of about one mile an hour. As she turned a corner, her car fishtailed and skidded sideways into a ditch. One tire was stuck in a sewer drain. Laurel wasn't hurt, but she was badly shaken. She didn't have a cell phone and had no idea how far she'd have to walk to get to a pay phone. She felt her heart starting to slam, but thought, *There's gotta be some help out there somewhere.* She stepped outside her car and looked around. Suddenly "a tall, strapping young man" of about seventeen or eighteen walked out of the nearby woods toward her. He didn't say a word. He waved at Laurel to get back into the car.

Then, Laurel said, "He proceeded to lift the car right out of the ditch. He put it down several inches from where it had been stuck, which gave me the traction to get going. I stopped for a few seconds to get out of the car to thank him but he was gone. Gone! He'd simply disappeared! I'll never forget that young man."

It took Laurel two more hours to get home (a distance of a few miles), but she arrived safely. "Sometimes I wonder if I dreamed the whole thing," Laurel said. "I mean, maybe he really *was* an angel . . ."

Look, I don't know if my Dan Blodgett or Laurel's strapping young man were real angels or not, whatever that means, but I do know that she and I had something in common: We let go of thinking we were completely alone and had to manage everything by ourselves, and we looked for help. Actually, we did more than that: We *anticipated* that we would *get* help.

I saw a woman do the same thing on a New York subway train the other day. And if you've ever ridden New York's subways, you know that the incident was its own kind of miracle. A woman got on a very crowded subway train and was carrying her purse and a large shopping bag filled to overflowing with groceries. I'm sure she would much rather have been sitting than standing as the train jerked along the track; I know I would have, and all I was carrying was my work bag. But she did something I didn't do: She looked around expectantly with a pleasant smile on her face—and raised her eyebrows slightly, as if she anticipated that someone was watching and would give up his or her seat. And someone *was* watching. Almost immediately a young man stood up and offered her his seat. She smiled again, thanked him warmly, and sat down. *Wow, I* thought. *Talk about anticipating angels!* I mean, she wasn't old, she wasn't crippled, she wasn't even drop-dead gorgeous. But she had this extraordinary kind of spirit about her that seemed to cause people to want to help. Honestly, if I'd been sitting I would have given her my seat. But she could have given off a very different aura—one of needing no help from anyone, one of being able to manage herself, one of assuming that no one would help her even if she asked for it. *There's really something to learn here,* I thought.

And as it turns out, this really is a big letting-go for me. It's right there near the top of my Mental Throwaways. And like a lot of the things on that list, I have to think about it almost every day or else I'm in danger of falling back into my old, defeating I've-got-to-do-it-all-by-myself habit.

Here's something that helps me discover more angels in my life: *being* an angel. My agent, Richard Pine, told me a story recently about a chance he got to be an angel. And he took it.

Late last summer as he was winding up a long, wonderful, late-afternoon walk in the Rockefeller preserve in northern Westchester County, he came upon a group of four people—middle-aged parents, their teenage daughter, and another woman in her forties. "They were extremely distraught," Richard said. "I asked if they were okay, and the man answered in heavily accented English that they were lost. They'd arrived about five hours earlier and although they had a map, they couldn't find their way back to where they'd parked their car. They were absolutely terrified."

Richard took a look at their map and realized that they'd parked their car about a thirty-minute walk from where they were standing. He also knew that the sun would soon set and that there would have been absolutely no way to make it back there before dark. "No wonder they were nervous and scared," he said. "I told them everything would be okay and that I'd drive them back to their car. They couldn't believe it. They'd thought they were going to have to spend the night in the woods, without food or water; they were afraid they might not be found for days."

After he dropped them off and they'd said their good-byes, Richard said he'd realized that somehow he'd been lucky enough to be a minor angel—a stranger who, at dusk, appeared out of nowhere and delivered them to safety." All these months later, Richard still hasn't gotten over his good fortune—the chance to be an angel. "I know I'd somehow been able to grant them their greatest wish—safety—but they'd granted mine as well: the opportunity to have a really positive impact on someone else's life." Richard's committed to discovering more angel moments. "All we have to do is be open to the opportunity to do good and be generous." he told me. "If we are, the opportunities will present themselves in abundance."

Of course, Richard is right. A few days after he told me his story, I had a small angel moment—and it made my day. A very rainy day, actually. I had just had my hair blown at my little neighborhood salon because I was going to give a speech at a major financial institution in a couple of hours, and I was walking down Madison Avenue looking for a cab. I put up my umbrella to try to shield my newly coiffed hair, but a gust of wind came along and turned it inside out. Plus, there were no cabs in sight. I tried to walk underneath the awnings of the boutiques that lined the avenue, but it didn't help. My hair, never mind my outfit, was getting ruined. And then, out of the blue, a cab stopped right in front of me. "Yessss!" I said out loud. The door opened and a lovely, elderly woman peeked out. "My, it's raining hard, isn't it?" she asked. "It sure is," I said. "I hope you don't have far to go." "I don't," she said, "I'm just going into the bank across the street, but I have a lot of things to bring with me."

As she struggled to get out of the cab, I saw that she had not only a large purse, but also a shopping bag and an oxygen tank. The oxygen tube was plugged into her nose. In one hand she had her purse and shopping bag and with the other hand she groped for the handle of the tank—with a lighted cigarette in her hand. "Let me get that for you," I said, grabbing hold of the oxygen tank and trying to keep it a healthy distance from her cigarette.

"That's very kind of you," she said and smiled a beautiful smile. I helped her out of the taxi, put the oxygen tank on the sidewalk next to her, and said, "I'd better help you across the street, the wind is blowing pretty hard." "But you'll miss your taxi," she said. And with that, the cabdriver said, "Sorry, I can't wait, miss. There are a million people looking for cabs." And he pulled away. "That's okay," I said. "I'm glad to help. You remind me of another lovely woman I knew—my mother." "Did she smoke?" the woman asked apropos of nothing. "Always," I replied, "even when she was on oxygen." "Well, God bless her," she said. I helped her across the street with the wind and rain blasting at us and ushered her into the bank. As I turned to leave, she put her hand on my arm and said, "Your mom must have been a wonderful woman—because you're an angel." "Why, thanks," I said. "She sure was."

That was it. It stopped raining. The wind died down and, although I had to walk about a dozen blocks, I finally found a cab. My hair was all over the place and my outfit looked a bit worse for the wear, but I felt good. The speech went fine, and when Jim asked me later that night how my day had gone, I said, "Actually, really, really good. I had a little angel moment that made my day." I told him about the woman with the oxygen tank and he said, "That's really nice. Reminds me of your mother."

So listen, if you're one of those people who assumes she's alone, who takes for granted that she has to handle everything herself, who sometimes, as a result, tips over into the (yuck) "martyr" category, this is the time to let it go. You're not alone. Not by a long shot. There are lots of really wonderful people out there who would like nothing better than to make your day. If you look up for a minute, you'll probably see one.

Never doubt the existence of angels. Look for them, anticipate them, count on them. Be one.

And if you run into a terrific guy named Dan Blodgett, tell him he's started a whole angel movement, will you? And tell him I haven't forgotten him.

Steps for finding the angels in your life:

1. Abandon your old conviction that you're alone, that the *only* one who can get it done is you, that you've got to figure everything out yourself. Make a list of those situations where you've always thought you had to do it all by yourself. Throw them all out.

2. Assume that there are wonderful people out there who would like nothing better than to lend you a hand or even save your bacon. Keep your eyes and ears open so that you don't miss them when they show up—or mistake them for someone else. People have a tendency to turn up when they're expected.

3. Take every opportunity you can to be someone's angel. Absolutely nothing will make you feel more worthy. Nothing.

4. Tell other people that we're starting an angel movement. Ask them to come along. The world's been waiting for thousands of years for us to show up.

Gail's Throw-Out Scorecard:

I will throw out that I'm alone, that I'm the only one that can make it happen.

Total: 1 thing
Running Total: 50 things (yeah, baby!)

Your Throw-Out Scorecard:

_____

_____

_____

_____

_____

_____

Your Total:
Your Running Total:

Chapter **20**	# Making It to Fifty: The Celebration

S o how does it feel? You've let go of a lot. You've thrown out everything from your old lipsticks to your fear of not being good enough—from your aunt's really unattractive china to the need to have everybody like you—from your too-tight belt to your too-small view of yourself.

Seriously, do you feel lighter, maybe even ebullient? I bet you've thrown out a lot more than fifty things. Have you got it all written down? Have you congratulated yourself and shared your list with someone else? Have you encouraged them to throw out their stuff and make their own list? It would be wonderful if you would log on to www.throwoutfiftythings.com to post your throw-outs, tell us your stories, and help us celebrate: you.

I'd love you to tell us what the hardest thing was for you to throw out. Was it a physical or an emotional thing? It's funny how the two are connected, isn't it? Whatever it was, you should be really proud that you did it. If you can do that, imagine what else you can do.

This is just the beginning. From now on, you're going to be vigilant. From now on, when you take a look at the stuff you've surrounded yourself with—or the mental debris that's begun to pile up again in your mind—you're going to ask these vital questions: Does it make me happy? Do I need it? Is this what I want to pass on? If you can't answer yes, you'll let it go. You've got the courage now, and the will.

So now that the decks are clear, now that the mental and physical arteries are unblocked, what would you like to have happen next? What would *good* look like for you? Guess what? You get to decide. Turn the page.

✢

PART FOUR

Stepping into the Clearing

Chapter 21

Your Vision for the Future

So here's the question: *Who are you now?* Now that you've let go of all the extraneous marble, now that you've chiseled your way through the stuff, junk, and clutter of your life, now that you've thrown out fifty things, who are you? Or more important, who do you want to be? The fact is, this is the moment to decide what your own idea of *good* is. This is the moment to decide what you look like—to yourself and to the world. At this particular moment, it's all up for grabs—nothing's given, nothing's decided, nothing's written until you write it.

There must have been moments, even days, weeks, or months, when Michelangelo agonized over who David was, what he represented, what point his existence would make. To know what was superfluous, what to take away from that multi-ton block of marble must have seemed, at times, bewildering. But of course, Michelangelo wasn't chiseling away willy-nilly, was he? He had a vision. A beautiful vision. Not, I'm sure, a "set-in-stone" (if you'll pardon the expression) vision, but a somewhat fluid, opportunistic one. Like every great artist in any medium, I'd imagine Michelangelo was always listening to what the marble was telling him, always responding to and considering slightly different directions, an alternative way of expressing David's uniqueness. But nevertheless, he had a vision, a drawing, however rough initially, to build upon, to guide him, to reveal to the world—and most certainly, ultimately, to reveal to himself.

It takes a vision to give us the resolve and the determination we need to make positive changes in our lives. **Nothing really big, really bold, or really beautiful was ever created in a country, in a company, in a family, or in a life without a vision—a clear picture of what *good* would look like, of how, if anything were possible, it would be.**

Walt Disney was a pretty smart guy, and he knew what it took to motivate people to create miracles—or at least *magic*. So when he created the Magic Kingdom, in Florida, he said to the executives planning the theme park, "Build the castle first!" Disney knew that the castle was where the magic was—and that if everyone working on the project had the castle to look to, in all its glory and magnificence, they could do all the hard stuff it took to bring the rest of the park to life. They could lay the cables in the swamps and all the heat and mosquitoes in the world wouldn't stop them. *Because here's what Disney taught us: If you can feel the magic, you can go the distance. Every time.*

So the question is this: What's your vision? What's

your castle? What would a drop-dead-good-as-it-gets life look like?

Look, we live in a world where information, not vision, is king. Most of us don't spend five minutes in a week (or a month, for that matter, or how about a year?) asking ourselves what *good* would look like in our lives. We spend a lot of time collecting data, studying the trends, assessing the risks, and plotting the time lines—but for what? For the next baby step we're considering taking to reach the corner, not the castle. It's hard to be bold without a vision. Everything looks like work without a vision. It's no wonder we get bogged down in the *processes* of life. Without the promise of magic at the end of the tunnel, it's hard to see the light.

But not anymore. Now that we're free of all those self-imposed shackles, we can finally flex our cramped-up muscles and step onto the field of play. So what's your vision? Look, your answer to this question doesn't have to be a forever answer. It just has to be today's answer. Take a couple of minutes to jot down some thoughts, will you? Would you be a published author, would you be a racecar driver? (I know a woman who brought that very vision to life.) Would you be walking down a golden beach holding on to the tiny hands of your grandchildren? Actually, that's my vision. Or one of them. (I have several, and when you get going with the vision thing, you will, too.) But here's my favorite: It's maybe five years from now (less would be good) and I see myself running along this beautiful beach holding the hands of Kate's and Abigail's children—my future grandchildren. And I'm walking along that beach with love and energy and humor and immense gratitude. Now, if I'm going to be walking along that beach, I've got to be here, right? And I've got to have energy. And that's the vision that gets me up every morning at six fifteen, in rain, sleet, and dark of night, to run around the reservoir in Central Park—in spite of or maybe because of my double bypass heart surgery, or "heart caper," as I refer to it. It's the vision that tells me what to do—eat healthily, work out regularly, take my meds, keep an optimistic attitude—and what not to do, or what to let go of: potato chips, ice cream, crossing my legs for long periods of time (can cause blood clots), getting worked up about the little stuff. In a word, that vision helps me keep two ongoing lists: WHAT TO KEEP and WHAT TO THROW OUT. And in my own case both lists are really long and, with luck and vigilance, will only get longer. *Never underestimate the power of a vision to guide your hand, your heart, and your mind.*

I can hear you say, "But Gail, I don't have a vision. I have absolutely no idea of what I really want or what *good* would look like for me!" Relax. It's okay. Now that we've cleared away the debris, the good will emerge. Honest. And amazingly, for many people I've worked with—and even for myself—once it's been discovered, the answer, the vision, seems so obvious, we can't imagine why we didn't see it before. Now that we've stepped out of the swamp of mental and physical clutter, we can see where the sun's coming from. Meanwhile, here are a couple of exercises to help you get a little more in touch with your David.

Vision Exercises:

- You're at a party where you don't know anyone and you're feeling slightly awkward, wondering why you came, and thinking about how soon you can leave without being rude. Out of the blue, you overhear a conversation among several people a few feet away. They're talking about something so compelling, so seductive, so intriguing that, despite your feeling shy, you go straight up to them and say, "Excuse me, but I couldn't help overhearing you talk about _____ and I just had to come over and introduce myself." What are they talking about? Raising golden retrievers? A cooking school in Tuscany? How to get your own television talk show? How to turn your newly uncluttered house totally green? Whatever that is, whatever would make you get over feeling shy and get into feeling bold, that's a big, fat hint about what could light up the next great segment of your life.

- You're at another gathering, but again you don't know anyone, and again you're wondering why the heck you came. This time, however, someone comes up to you and asks, "So what are *you* up to?" And you're thrilled to hear yourself say, "Well, I'm very much involved with _____. And I couldn't be happier." "Wow," the other person says, "I wish I were doing something I loved that much!" Okay, so what was your answer? You've started taking acting classes? You've created a cookbook and a cooking school for kindergartners? You were just accepted as a contestant on *Jeopardy!*?

Here's the point: Let yourself get carried away. (Where have you heard that before?) Let yourself imagine something that thrills you. Not something that necessarily seems logical or even doable at the moment; but something that, if it were to happen, you'd be the happiest person in town. Something that would light you up so much, you'd do just about anything to make it happen.

A woman I started coaching years ago decided at the age of forty-seven that she wanted to make a major career change. Michelle had spent more than twenty years running a nonprofit organization that provided housing to senior citizens. While she loved the work and its heart-warming results, she was ready to try something new. In fact, she harbored a secret, a decades-old longing to become an entertainment lawyer. Lawyering ran deep in her family. Michelle's father was a retired judge, and her brother was a prosecuting attorney. But Michelle had never been encouraged to go to law school by her parents and had assumed they thought she didn't have the right stuff. They, on the other hand, had assumed she wasn't interested. As it turned out, both of those assumptions couldn't have been farther from the truth. (Boy, you've got to watch out for those assumptions, they'll get you every time.) Now Michelle just needed the courage to bring her passion to life.

So we spent some time creating a vision—Michelle's "castle." She imagined what her days would be like, what parts of the country her work might take her to, the intellectual caliber of her colleagues, and, most important, a deadline for reaching her goal. By the time we were finished, Michelle could almost reach out and touch her desk in the law firm where she would be working one day.

When Michelle announced she was applying to law school, her husband was completely shocked. "Are you kidding?" he said. "Do you know how old you'll be when you graduate? Fifty!"

"I'll be fifty anyway," she replied.

Three years ago, Michelle graduated (yes, at age fifty),

and she is now working as an associate in a Washington, DC, firm that specializes in the field of entertainment law. She's working hard, and she's loving it. Her husband, who moved with her, is extraordinarily proud of her and is happily designing his own major career change—at age fifty-six.

Of course, your vision doesn't have to be all about your career or even your health. *All it has to be is bold.* At a workshop I conducted a couple of years ago, a woman named Isabel had one of my all-time favorite visions. She decided to create a relationship in which she and her soon-to-be husband would fall more in love every year. She wrote down how each of them would feel about the other at the end of year one and at the end of year two, year three, and so on. Then she wrote down exactly how they would create that feeling together. She thought of small ways to let him know how terrific he was: humorous, affectionate e-mails in the middle of the day for no particular reason; toasts over a glass of wine at night to celebrate any small, good thing that had happened. She created a terrific concept she called "You're with Me Tonight!": surprise dates where each of them would take turns wowing the other with new, out-of-the-way restaurants, obscure movies, or moonlight swims.

Isabel e-mailed me a few weeks ago to tell me that she and her husband had already reached their castle. In fact, she said, "We added a new wing!" The addition of a new baby girl is bringing them even closer together. Isabel and her husband learned something invaluable: If they could dream it, they could do it. And by the way, the "You're with Me Tonight!" events are still happening. Maybe not as frequently, but a tradition's a tradition.

So it's time to build your castle. What would it look like? How would it feel? Flesh it out; color it in. Put in every little flag, tower, and turret. I can see my grandchildren; I can hear them laughing; I can see the sun shining on their hair and the sturdiness of their little bodies. Nothing in my control will keep me from being there with them. I love cheeseburgers and potato chips, but I won't eat them. I hate lifting weights, but I'll lift them. In fact, I can't think of any annoyance or inconvenience I won't endure to be able to run along that beach, holding those little hands.

Now it's your turn. How good could you make it?

Steps to creating a vision of your new David:

1. Ask yourself this question: *If absolutely anything were possible, if I knew I couldn't fail, if a genie popped out of a bottle and said he'd grant my fondest wish, what would it be?* What would light you up so much, you'd be willing to do anything, short of selling your soul, to make it happen?

2. Don't be practical; you can always play small. This is the time to play big.

3. Flesh out your vision; build the castle. Put in all the details you can imagine, the wings, turrets, flags, and towers. If it's starting a new business, what is your typical day like? If it's finding the person of your dreams, what is it about your soul mate that stirs your heart? If it's getting fit once and for all, how do you feel when you walk into that restaurant wearing that new dress, swinging those toned-up arms, smiling that drop-dead smile?

4. Set a date. Be specific about when your vision will become a reality. Not just the year, but the month and the exact day. And don't make it more than eighteen months into the future. You've waited long enough. It's time to get what you want.

Chapter 22

Taking Energy From Your Defining Moments

Okay, this is really important. This is one of the places where the rubber meets the road; this is one of those moments when you really get it about my favorite word, *deciding*. There are so many opportunities in our lives—several every day, if we're vigilant—to decide what it'll be, how it'll go, what we're made of. And in the end, it all comes down to a moment—sometimes to nothing more than a split second—when we opt to move forward or shrink back.

I ask virtually everyone I work with—executives, entrepreneurs, entertainers, people between careers, between marriages, between an old self and a new self, and people who are just plain worried that they don't have the stuff or the right to get what they really want—to make a list of the defining moments in their lives. **A defining moment is an occasion when you found something in yourself you didn't know you had, or forgot you had, and pulled it out. And as a result, you changed an outcome from negative to positive.** A defining moment is when you said, "Yes, I will," or "No, I won't." A defining moment is when you drew a line. Or erased one, if that's what needed to be done. But it's always a moment after which you never think of yourself in quite the same way again. We all have them. In fact, I bet if you took a good look, you'd come up with a ton of them.

And that's what I'd like you to do: Start thinking about the moments—little and big—that, as you look back at them, make you say, "Hmmm, so *that's* who I am." They don't have to be the time you cured world hunger or stuck your finger in the dike and prevented the Great Flood. But they do have to be those times when you showed your inner pluck, said what had to be said, did what had to be done, and got on with it. Remember David Hoffman, the documentary filmmaker we talked about in chapter 10? David lost everything, every representation of his past work in that terrible fire. He could have chosen, as he put it, to come to a "dead stop" or to "keep going." He knew that was his defining moment. And he chose to move forward.

Here are a few examples from some other wonderful people I know, to get you started.

Christa, a young woman in her early thirties, told me this story recently. She was about to get married; in fact her wedding was only a week away—and her father announced that he refused to escort her down the aisle. A little background: Her father had left Christa and her mother when she was only ten years old. He remarried quite quickly to a woman who, unfortunately, was jealous of Christa as she grew up and threw all sorts of barriers in the way of her father spending time with her. Her father didn't fight back. Actually, he acquiesced. As a result Christa rarely saw him.

Christa's mom had eventually remarried a wonderful guy who took very naturally to the role of stepfather and staunch supporter of Christa. She grew to love him very much, to the exclusion of her own dad (whose behavior she always forgave). Twenty years later, when Christa and her husband-to-be were making the final arrangements for their wedding, she invited both her dad and her stepfather to escort her down the aisle. Her stepfather was thrilled. Her dad was outraged. He called her and said, "Do you have any idea how embarrassing it would be to walk down the aisle in front of all those people with another man who's not even a relative of yours? How could you be so selfish? What would make you even think of such a mean, destructive thing to do? If he's going to walk you down the aisle, count me out. You have to choose." Christa had always been the arbiter in her family, always the one to smooth things out between her parents, always the one to overlook her own feelings or to give in, to make it okay for someone else.

The last two difficult decades floated in front of her eyes. There had been a lot of bad parts, but there had been good parts, too. "How do I hang onto the good and throw out the rest?" she wondered.

"By telling the truth," her own voice responded. And at that moment, something new snapped into place. Call it resolve, call it courage, call it an instinct to trade in the past for the future—whatever it was, it worked. Christa gathered herself up and said these brave words to her father:

"Do you have any idea how much it hurt when you walked out on Mom and me? Do you know how embarrassing it was to try to explain that at school? Do you know how many hockey games and school plays and good and bad moments you missed in my life? Do you know that my stepdad is the one who was *there*? My stepdad is the one who packed my school lunches and wiped my eyes when my feelings were hurt and dropped everything to help me with my homework, or anything else I needed help with. My stepdad was there through it all—and I love him very much. But I love you, too. You're my dad. And this will be the most important day in my life. I'd like you to walk me down the aisle, but only if you can join my stepdad. *You* have to choose."

Christa's father was dumbfounded. Actually, he was speechless. Suddenly he said, "I'll be there. I'm sorry. I didn't realize . . ." He was in tears. Well, it all worked out. Both Christa's dad and her stepdad walked her down the aisle and it truly was not only one of the most important but also one of the happiest days in her life. Looking back at the moment, Christa, who had almost forgotten to tell me the story, realized that this truly was a moment that defined her—to herself. "My God," I said, "do you have any idea how strong you are? Do you realize what courage you have? If you can do that, you can do anything." "I know now," Christa said.

Now, if you're saying to yourself, or out loud for that matter, "Hey, Gail, I don't have any moments like that" —think again. Think about my dear friend, Ray Sclafani. He's a hardworking, self-starter kind of guy who gets it done. But when I asked him to go home and make a list of the defining moments in his life, he balked. "I can't do that," he said. "I don't have time, with my work and my family"—he has very young kids—"and anyway, I don't have any defining moments." "Just do it, Ray," I said. And he did. He came back two weeks later with five pages of defining moments. Once he started, he couldn't stop. "I'm just worried about all the ones I missed!" he said. "Don't worry," I told him. "There'll be a whole lot more."

What kick-started the process for Ray was remembering when he'd run for class president in the ninth grade. He'd run his heart out. And he lost. But he still had to go to school the next day. He still had to walk down the same halls. He still had to say hi to the same kids. And he'd done it. What he'd found in himself was the will and, yes, the courage to keep his small, fourteen-year-old self going. When we talked about the episode, we realized that it really was a good thing that Ray had lost that election because if he'd won, he wouldn't have learned half as much about himself. "You know, when I think about it, just that one little memory reminds me of how strong I am and that whatever comes along, I can handle it." Yes, he can. Ray recently launched his own company, ClientWise, that provides cutting-edge training for financial advisers and other key executives. It's doing great.

Ray has become a true collector of defining moments in his life, as well as in the lives of his wife and children. Seriously, he chronicles moments for everybody, and they celebrate them from time to time. We do the same in our family. Every Christmas Eve, Jim, Kate, Abigail, and I relate our own and one another's defining moments from the last year. Sometimes it's hilariously funny. Sometimes it brings us to tears. But it always, always reminds us—as individuals and as a family—who we are and what we're made of.

Are you thinking of some moments of your own yet? I bet you are. But here's one last story to spur you on. It's one I dredged up about myself. It's funny but I wouldn't have thought about it if I hadn't listened to Ray tell his story about losing the election in the ninth grade . . .

It happened at a two-day regional swim competition conducted by the Amateur Athletic Union as a qualifying event for the Women's Nationals the following month. Here's the thing: You couldn't get to the nationals if you didn't do well in the regionals, and you couldn't do well in your region if you didn't get into the finals. That meant you had to have a really fast time in your qualifying heat. My race was the twelve-and-under girls' fifty-meter freestyle.

"Judges and timers ready?" said the starter. "Swimmers, take your marks!" We all stepped onto our starting blocks, crouched in the start position, and waited for the gun. I focused straight ahead, staring at the other end of the fifty-meter pool. The water glistened in the hot Indiana sun. My heart slammed.

I heard my mom yell, "Okay, Gail, you can do it, sweetie." The starter cocked his gun. And then an odd thing happened. The girl in the lane next to mine teetered back and forth a couple of times. I thought she was going to fall into the water, which would have been considered a false start. But she didn't. I did! Watching her, I had thrown myself off balance and fallen feetfirst into the pool just as the gun was fired. I stood there in the shallow end as the other swimmers barreled toward the finish, looked up at the judge, and shouted, "Hey, that was a false start!"

"No, it wasn't," he said.

"But, but, it... I..."

"Sorry," he said with a shrug.

I started to cry. Then I started to swim. I swam and cried all the way down the pool. I can still feel my arms tearing through that water and my feet kicking as if they had a life of their own. I gave one final burst of speed and slammed my hand onto the tiles at the finish. Then I looked up, still crying. The timer yelled, "Number two!" I realized I'd managed by a hairbreadth to come in second. My coach, Bob Busby, grabbed my arm and pulled me out of the pool and said, "That was beautiful, really beautiful. I've never seen you move so fast." Actually, he'd never seen me so mad.

"But I only got second," I said.

"I wouldn't care if you'd come in fifth!" he said. "It was beautiful." My time was good enough to get me into the finals later that day, and I was so motivated and energized (and still mad) that I took first place. It's funny, but no one ever talked much about that first-place medal. It was "crying and swimming all the way to second place" that they remembered. I've been in plenty of seemingly unfair, come-from-behind situations in my life since that hot July day in Indiana. But I know what to do. I just ask myself this: *So what'll it be, Gail? Quit or swim?* And I can tell you, swimming always feels better. Even if I come in second. *Or third. Or whatever.*

So what'll it be for you? What will you decide? What will enable you to keep moving forward when it seems like almost everything in the world is moving against you, when it's not fair, or fun, and you've just lost the election? What will you choose? Quit or swim? You know the answer.

Steps for celebrating how courageous you already are:

1. Look back to when you were little, to yesterday—for those moments when you found something in yourself you didn't know you had and pulled it out. When you said, "Here's how it's going to go . . ." Make a list of those moments, both big and small.

2. Look for the pattern. You'll see that there were times when you made a decision against all flags; when you stood up for yourself—or someone else; when you moved forward despite the odds. A pattern will emerge. The pattern is called "courage."

3. Celebrate these moments. Share them with someone you love. Ask them to share theirs as well.

4. Commit to keeping a running list of your defining moments and to reviewing them on a regular basis—even when you're not faced with a major challenge or crisis. It's an incredibly energizing habit. Don't break it.

Chapter 23 | Being Unforgettable

So here's the really good news. In addition to all the other things we get to decide—what to let go of (the mental and physical debris of our lives), what to keep (the moments of courage that defined us), what *good* looks like to us (the castle that we're building, the vision we're bringing to life), what makes us unique (if enough people love us, the ones who don't, don't matter)—we also get to decide, at any given moment, what people think of us.

Boy, I wish I'd realized that a whole lot earlier. I thought for decades that other people would think whatever they thought about me, regardless of what I did. I didn't know that I was totally in charge of their perception; that I could, at any moment, change my act, and therefore change their perception.

As I've said a million times, "The Universe hasn't made its mind up about you. It only knows what you show it today." Our actress friend Teri proved that, didn't she? Against all stereotypes, she wowed her class with her own surprisingly convincing version of Juliet. And as you recall, it was her *conviction* that she was Juliet that persuaded us and gave us no choice but to buy her act. Now you get to decide. How do you want to come across? How do you want to present yourself? What impression do you want to create—when you walk into a room, up to a microphone, into an interview, or onto the stage? What do you want them to remember about you?

Communicating who you are *now* is as important as *designing* your persona. If people don't get it about you, it's not their fault; it's yours. But presenting your new self to any audience, large or small, with power and grace can be a daunting proposition. According to the List of Most Common Fears, the fear of public speaking ranks ahead of the fear of dying. So that means that most people would rather die than speak in public. Does that make you laugh? Good. And don't worry, presenting yourself powerfully and authentically isn't hard. In fact, it's a joy. How do I know? My father taught me. And I can teach you.

"Hiya, gorgeous." That's what my father said as he stepped out of a yellow convertible on parents' weekend at Camp Farwell in Newbury, Vermont. I threw my arms around his neck and started to cry. I loved my dad—and my mom—so much it hurt. They were Fred and Ginger; they were Scott and Zelda; they were even, at times, George and Gracie. And they made me feel as if I could do anything, even withstand the overwhelming homesickness I'd been experiencing for the last four weeks. I still remember what my mom was wearing—a white flannel skirt, a navy-blue sweater with horses on it, blue-and-white spectators. I have no idea what my dad was wearing. I only know how he made me feel: like I was the only person in the world. Just looking at him could perk a girl up. He was fabulously handsome, a blend of Cary Grant and Gary Cooper, with a grin you could see a mile away. And he carried himself with the power of an athlete and the grace of a dancer. He was unforgettable.

My rank on the camp popularity scale skyrocketed within hours of my parents' arrival. The counselors, who hadn't paid much attention to me before, couldn't get enough of me. "Will you introduce me to your dad—I mean, your parents—Gail?" was the question I heard over and over. They all said my dad had "charisma." I didn't know what that meant, so when my parents took me out to dinner that night, I asked my father. He thought about it for a few minutes and said, "I think charisma is passion demonstrated. It's when you let your enthusiasm and optimism show and use your energy to inspire the next fella."

My dad had an uncanny ability to "inspire the next fella," and I've used his techniques for doing that in hundreds of situations: on first dates, in speeches, in job interviews. I've also taught his techniques to many of the people I coach who, like you, are ready to step into the light. I remember watching him at sales meetings at a door-to-door vacuum cleaner company he ran in Cleveland. He was mesmerizing. He could transform the energy in any room from exhausted to exuberant in minutes. He believed that people were capable of achieving their wildest dreams and that his job was to help them.

How did he do it? He let his passion show. He didn't hold back. He was willing to look foolish if it meant getting his point across and moving "the next fella" to action. He never taught or preached (although he was related to the turn-of-the-century orator and presidential candidate William Jennings Bryan). He was a passionate listener. He knew instinctively that the greatest way to pay respect to anyone—a child, an elderly person, someone on top of the world, or someone in pain—is to listen. He also knew that the old saying is right: People don't care how much you know until they know how much you care.

You're going to laugh at this but before I went to Yale Drama School, I'd never played a girl's part. I'm not kidding. (You're wondering how I got accepted to that venerable institution, aren't you? It remains a puzzle to this day.) Look, as I said when we were in the living room (chapter 4), I went to a women's college and I was always cast as the male lead. In addition to playing the devil in *Damn Yankees* (my favorite part), I played Woody in *Finian's Rainbow* (I sang "That Old Devil Moon" to my roommate) and Bottom in *A Midsummer Night's Dream* (a raucous, rollicking part). It was all good fun.

But the drama school was a serious place, and my fellow students were not just fooling around. One of the first assignments was to walk out onto the stage and say who we were, where we were from, and what acting we had done. The audience, made up of all the other first-year drama school students, was instructed to vote on whether we were "heavy" or "light." I can tell you right now, it wasn't good to be light. Light meant you couldn't take the stage, that you didn't have presence or gravitas, that you weren't commanding. To be light was to be forgettable.

I called my dad the night before I had to go on. "I can't do this," I said. "I'll feel foolish. How can I tell them that I've played nothing but boys' parts? These people have done Off-Off Broadway. They're almost professional. They'll know I'm a lightweight."

"Okay, let's think this through," he said. "Here's what you're going to do: You're going to walk onto that stage with energy and optimism, anticipating that the audience is going to love you. And here's the big one: You're going to shift your attention from yourself to your audience." Now, that's probably one of the most important things my dad taught me about winning people over, and it works anytime you're trying to make a positive impression. Including a blind date. Don't think, *How'm I doing? Do they like me?* Think *How are they? What do they need?* Look out, not in. And then Dad said something I'll never forget. **"Great acting or great speaking—or just plain great communicating—is, at the risk of sounding corny, about love. You've got to love the audience so much that you'll do anything to get your idea or your message across. When they feel that,"** he said, **"they'll love you right back.** Oh," he said, "and don't forget to show 'em your passion."

So I walked out on that stage and did what he told me. I talked about how much I loved playing the devil, the kick I got out of "romancing" my roommate, and the great fun of playing Bottom. I made them laugh by telling them that I knew I was convincing when younger girls developed crushes on me. I concentrated on caring about—even loving—every student sitting in the theater. I got a standing ovation and, best of all, I was pronounced "heavy." Believe it or not, eventually I even got to play a girl.

My dad has been gone for a few years now, but I think about him every day. I think about the impact he had on people; I think about how he changed every room he walked into; about how magnetic and loving he was. Even now, when I walk down Euclid Avenue in Cleveland, inevitably someone will come up to me and say, "Hey, wasn't Warren Blanke your father? I heard him speak once. I'll never forget him." Neither will I.

So what about you? If you're going to bring your best self into the next great segment of your life, you've got to express yourself honestly, openly, and, yes, unforgettably, whether you're walking into a PTA meeting or a capacity crowd at the Waldorf. All evidence to the contrary, it's *not* hard to start loving it rather than hating it; it's *not* hard to go from mediocre to marvelous.

And the good news is: You don't have to be born with charisma; it can be acquired. It's all in your attitude. Thanks to a little help from my dad, here's how to get that unstoppable attitude.

Steps for presenting yourself powerfully and being unforgettable:

1. *Conviction.* You've got to believe that you are exactly the right person at the right place at the right time to be walking into this room, up to this microphone, into this interview, or onto this stage; that you are exactly the right person to be telling this story, making this pitch, asking for this order. And you are. You're free, you're clear, and you're unstoppable.

2. *Courage.* Stepping into the limelight takes courage. And you've got it. Take another look at your defining moments. Remember that you already have what it takes to be bold, to take a stand, to have a point of view. Before you speak, remind yourself of your finest moment, your best shot, the time you pulled it out of the fire. Walk in with that moment all over you. Wear it; own it; revel in it.

3. *Passion.* As my dad said, charisma is nothing more or less than passion demonstrated. Everything starts with passion. In the end, passion drives profits. Believe in your vision of what *good* looks like and let your passion show. We believe people who are passionate. We trust them. Simply put, passionate people are unforgettable—whether they're politicians, entrepreneurs, CEOs, singers, or stand-up comics. Passion wins.

4. *Let go.* Let go of any negative thoughts or fears of not being good enough; review your list of Fifty Things. Pay special attention to your Mental Throwaways. Let go of trying to be perfect or thinking you have to please everybody. Remember, if enough people love you, the ones who don't, don't matter.

5. *Shift your attention to your audience.* It's ironic, isn't it? It's not about you; it's about them. And that, my friend, is why you don't have to be nervous. Go from thinking, *How am I doing, do they like me, how do I look?* to *How are they doing, what do they need, how can I give that to them?* You'll feel your attention floating back to yourself from time to time; send it right back out there. Love the audience and they'll love you right back.

6. *Motivate and inspire.* Never teach or preach. Nobody really wants to be taught or lectured to. It's true: "People don't care how much you know until they know how much you care." The minute you catch yourself in a teaching mode, stop. A key difference between Hillary Clinton and Barack Obama when they were rival candidates in the 2008 Democratic primaries is that one "taught" and one "inspired." Guess which is which?

7. *Speak into the "listening" of your audience.* You've got to know what your audience is out for, whether it's one person or a whole roomful. What are they committed to? What worries them, delights them, moves

them? If you're asking for their approval, fashion your request as a means to bring *their* vision to life. When they know you get it about them, and understand what they want or are interested in, they'll relax and actually start listening to you. The moment that happens, you've got 'em.

8. *Anticipate that they'll love you.* Walk into every room with energy and optimism. Think Cher. Whenever she walks out onto the stage, she makes a fundamental decision that she'll connect. That the audience will know she loves them and that they'll love her right back. Exuding positive energy can turn the tide in your direction. Remember, this is your moment. Why shouldn't you win the day? Why should it be somebody else? You're worthy, you're ready, and you're *unforgettable.*

Chapter 24

Find Your Song— and Sing It!

Well, this is it. Remember when Michelangelo presented David to the fellow who had come to judge the quality of his latest work? I can imagine his flinging off the sheet that covered the statue with great fanfare. Okay, maybe he didn't say "Ta-daaah," but he was probably thinking it.

So this is *your* "Ta-daaah" moment. This is the moment when you once and for all fling off that sheet and step out of the marble; out of the debris of the past and into the bright light of the future—a future unfettered by regrets, fear of failure, missed opportunities, closed mind-sets, overstuffed closets, or dried-up tubes of Krazy Glue. A future of your own design where the ultimate seduction is a vision—your vision—of what drop-dead *good* looks like. This is the moment of the ultimate letting-go—when you let go of the safety of a self-imposed straitjacket and embrace the glorious insecurity of the unknown.

Are you ready? There's the drumroll. The orchestra

leader has raised his baton. The musicians are poised to play . . . your song. But wait, what are they going to play? What *is* your song, anyway? **You've got to have a song. I mean, has any band of brothers or sisters ever gone into battle, ever gone out to save the world, start a movement, or seize the day without a song? No, the bagpipes, the fifes and drums, the raised voices always went first. We all need a song.**

Actually, I believe so strongly in the power of a song that I ask every single one of my clients to find theirs. And sing it.

Finding your song isn't hard. This little story will help: Not long ago, I coached a forty-year-old guy named Roger who worked for an asset management company. His CEO had told him to beef up his communication skills. He came across to potential clients as bored and disinterested, even arrogant. But in reality, he was 100 percent committed and eager to make the sale. (It's interesting, isn't it, how frequently there's such a huge gap between our intention and the actual impact we produce.) But the great thing about Roger was that after he got over his initial shock at the unintended impression he created, he was one of the most willing students I've ever had—and "beefing up his communication skills" turned out to be a piece of cake.

Early in our conversations, Roger and I started to talk about sports. It turned out that he had been a star on his high school soccer team. We talked about his toughest game, the one that he had helped pull out of the fire to win the league championship and earn him the Most Valuable Player award. "What did you think about when you drove to the game?" I asked. "What did you think when you walked onto that field? Did you have a song you loved?"

"I can't believe you're asking me that," he said. "I did have a song. I played it on the way to every game and sang it in my head on the field. You're really going to crack up when I tell you what it was," he said.

"Go ahead, I can handle it," I said with a laugh.

"It was 'My Sharona' by the Knack. I loved it. It never failed to get my juices flowing."

"Well, that's the answer," I said. "'My Sharona.' Listen, you've got to understand that the work you do is just another kind of game. And the good news is, once again you've got the makings of an incredibly valuable player. You just need to have the same spirit and energy when you meet with a client as you had when you took that other field."

"Wait," he said. "You mean I should sing 'My Sharona'? You're kidding, right?"

"Nope," I replied. At this point I was so excited I'd stood up and was waving my arms around. "You've got to belt it out at the top of your lungs on the way to every single meeting and hear it in your head when you walk in. C'mon, are you game?"

Roger was game. And I know it sounds crazy, but

singing that silly song made all the difference. Roger came out of himself; he became a motivator. He energized his clients, and they loved it. Now he's the guy the CEO calls on when she wants to clinch a deal. And Roger delivers. And he did it all by recapturing a moment in his life when he felt unstoppable and by replaying the song that made him feel that way.

There's another fellow I know who's currently facing the biggest challenge of his life. In fact, he's *fighting* for his life. He has prostate cancer and is undergoing chemotherapy. He's gaining on his disease, and he feels one of the greatest tools in his arsenal is his positive energy and unyielding optimism. And he says he gets it from his song.

Before he goes in for a treatment, and even when he's actually undergoing a treatment, he hears it. It's the overture from *The Lion King,* and it does it for him every time. "You should hear me, Gail," he said, "I belt that baby out and I can feel my body responding with everything it's got. That's when I know I've got this thing licked."

It's a lot easier to be brave when you've got a song.

Easier to be irresistible, too. A darling young woman named Patti had been out of work for months and months. She'd had plenty of interviews but none had panned out—partly because the job in question wasn't really her cup of tea, partly because she just didn't exude the energy and optimism that many people are looking for during tough times. But finally, she found the perfect job. It was a senior coordinator's position at MTV, working on a show she really loved. The company had narrowed down their candidates to two, and the great news was that Patti was one of them. She was about to go for the final interview. "Ohmygod, Gail," she said, "I really, really want this. They've got to pick me. I'm so nervous! What should I do?"

"Well, of course, you've got to sing your song, Patti," I said. "Wait," she said, "what song? I don't have a song." "Of course you do," I said, "you just don't know it. C'mon, what's the song that perfectly describes the way you *want* to feel right now? You know, how much you know that you're the right person for this job, that you've waited long enough, that this is it, that you're—" "I got it," Patti said. "It's by Elton John. It's 'The Bitch Is Back.'"

"I think that's gonna do it," I said.

Patti sang her song at the top of her lungs all the way to the interview. She walked in owning her power, oozing confidence and positive energy. She was irresistible. "They had no choice," she told me afterward. "I was so hot, they had to hire me."

And they did.

Okay, I've got a song. I sing it when I'm ready to put it on the line, when there's a lot at stake, when I've got a great opportunity and I don't want to blow it—when I hear myself say, *Okay, don't let this be the time I mess up.*

It's from *Funny Girl* and it's called, "I'm the Greatest

Star." I heard Barbra Streisand sing it live a million years ago. "I'm the greatest star. I am by far, but no one knows it." Sometimes I sing it under my breath; sometimes I belt it out. And here are the killer words that set me right up, that get my adrenaline flowing, that remind me that I really am the right person to knock 'em dead: "Lookin' down you'll never see me. Try the sky, 'cause that'll be me . . ."

I sing my song every time I walk into a challenging, ego-on-the-line situation. And it always works. Oh, I don't mean I always make the sale or win the day. But I always bring my best self into the room—whether it's a media interview, a speech, or a cocktail party filled with people I don't know.

What would it take for you to know the truth: that you're exactly the right person, at the right place, at the right time, to get what you want? What song would you hear—and sing—when you've decided to be energized, irresistible, and unforgettable? Here's what it takes: You have to find your song and sing it. Sing it for all your worth. Why not? This is the moment you've been waiting for. And the world has been waiting *for you*—to step into the limelight. You—with all those flags flying. You—with all your newfound clarity and lightness of spirit. You—with your vision, your castle to propel you forward. You—with a song in your heart . . . and on your lips.

Curtain up.

Steps for finding your song . . . and singing it:

1. *Find it.* Think back to a moment in your life when you felt like a million bucks. Maybe you were on the bus in high school returning from a great softball game, or at a dance and that extremely cute guy pulled you out onto the dance floor. What were they playing? What were you singing? That's your song.

2. *Sing it.* Out loud if you can, or just to yourself in an elevator or on a busy street. (Actually, as I was jogging in Central Park this morning, a guy ran past me belting out something about a "new direction." It really got me pumped.) Sing it on the way to the interview, the big presentation, or the first date, or going to pick up the kids from school.

3. *Share it.* Ask someone you love what his or her song is, and tell them yours.

4. *Use it.* Remember, no matter how worried you are, no matter how far behind you're running, your song will get you there.

Chapter 25 | Your Declaration to the World

Because you're free and clear now, because you know who you are and what you stand for, because your energy and spirit are renewed, because you have gifts to give and the courage to give them, it's time to make your declaration to the world. It's time for you to come forward, without waiting to be invited, and state your purpose.

And it's time for you to complete these sentences:

- *I'm _____ and I'm the one who . . . and nobody does it better.*
- *My vision for myself and for the world is . . .*
- *The toughest and most important thing I'm going to let go of to make sure that happens is . . .*
- *And my song is . . .*

Now you're not only unforgettable but unstoppable.

Look at your declaration every day. Say it out loud every morning. This is your moment, my friend. Take it.

Appendix: Your Throw-Outs

✢

The Physical Clutter

Things I'm Throwing Out:

_____

_____

_____

_____

_____

Things I'm Donating:

_____

_____

_____

_____

_____

Things I'm Selling:

_____

_____

_____

Things I'm Recycling:

THE MENTAL MESS

Things I'm Throwing Out:

THE SPECIAL FINDS

Things I'm Keeping and Why:

_____

_____

_____

_____

_____

_____

_____

GRAND TOTAL

Things: _____

Resource Guide

✠

*O*nce you've gathered your fifty (or more!) things together, you'll want to get rid of them properly. Throughout this book I've tried to offer as many "green" solutions for donating, giving away, swapping, trading, recycling, and reusing, and you'll find more here in this resource guide. I've listed a number of national organizations that you can contact, and I'm sure more will be created between when I write and when the book comes out. Most recycling still happens on the local level, so if you're serious about disposing of your items in a way that's environmentally safe, I encourage you to check with your town, city, or state to find out what options you have in your community. In most places you can recycle metal, glass, plastic, and paper curbside, but here are some options for what to do with the rest!

HOW TO DONATE, RECYCLE, AND DISPOSE OF THE FIFTY THINGS YOU THROW AWAY

General Donations

Goodwill Industries International
www.goodwill.org
1 (800) 664-6577

Salvation Army will take any item (clothes, furniture, shoes) in good condition
www.salvationarmyusa.org
1 (800) 725-2769

Check local organizations like the Junior League, churches and synagogues, et cetera.

Bicycles

www.bikesfortheworld.org
www.recycleyourbicycle.com
www.workingbikes.org

Books

www.booksforsoldiers.com
Your local public schools and libraries
Used-book stores in your area

Building Materials

Build It Green reuses old appliances, doors, and unused building materials
www.builditgreen.org

Sustainable ABC.com is a Web site devoted to exploring the relationship between ecology and sustainability
www.sustainableabc.com

Ecologue—easier ways to live green
www.ecologue.com

Cell Phones

www.cellphonesforsoldiers.com
www.charitablerecycling.com
www.recellular.com
www.wadv.org (Women Against Domestic Violence)

Clothing

How to Donate Clothing to a Homeless Shelter
www.ehow.com/how_10125_donate-clothing-homeless.html

American Red Cross and We Collect Clothes
www.wecollectclothes.com

Planet Aid
www.planetaid.org

Used sneakers
- Reuse-A-Shoe
www.letmeplay.com/reuseashoe

Gently used women's professional clothing, including shoes and handbags
- Women's Alliance (in 21 states)
www.thewomensalliance.org
- Dress for Success (in 37 states)
www.dressforsuccess.org

Used prom and other formal dresses, purses, shoes, jewelry
- The Princess Project
www.princessproject.org
- Glass Slipper Project
http://glassslipperproject.org

Used wedding dresses
- Brides Against Breast Cancer
www.bridesagainstbreastcancer.org

Catholic Charities
www.catholiccharitiesusa.org

Electronics

Lists of recyclers
www.techsoup.org
www.electronicsrecycling.org

Rechargeable batteries
- Drop off at your local Radio Shack
www.radioshackcorporation.com/cc/environmental
.html
- Rechargeable Battery Recycling Corporation
www.rbrc.org

Computers
- For a ten-dollar charge, your local Staples store will
disassemble for recycling
- Local senior centers are always looking for working
computers

Environmentally Sensitive Materials

www.epa.gov/garbage
Your local recycling center or landfill
Your city or state environmental regulatory
department

Food Items

Find local food banks for your unused pantry items at:
- America's Second Harvest, including a food bank
locator
www.secondharvest.org
- National Hunger Clearinghouse
www.worldhungeryear.org
- The Salvation Army
www.salvationarmyusa.org

Junk Mail

The Direct Mail Marketing Association can help you reduce the amount of junk mail that comes into your house (and I'll let you count it as one of your throwaways in advance) by showing you how to get your name off mailing lists

www.dmachoice.org

Office

Printer Cartridges/Toner
- Cartridge World

www.cartridgeworldusa.com
- Drop off at stores like Office Depot, Staples, and Best Buy

Digitizing your books and files
- SiftSort

www.siftsort.com

Various Goods

Freecycle Network:
www.freecycle.org
4,361 groups with 5,094,282 people (as of this writing) giving and getting items for free. Membership is free but you must join to participate. Each local group is moderated by a local volunteer.

Freesharing.org:
825 locally managed groups serving 350,000 members in the United States and others worldwide
www.freesharing.org

FoodShare.us: The goal is to give people a means to donate perishable and nonperishable food that might otherwise go to waste
www.freesharing.org/foodshare.php

Selling Your Things Online

Craigslist
www.craigslist.org

eBay
www.ebay.com

Go Antiques
www.goantiques.com

Parting with Possessions
www.partingwithpossesions.com
(410) 337-0085

Find a local consignment shop
www.consignmentshops.com

Trading Your Things

BarterBee
www.barterbee.com

Care-to-Trade
www.caretotrade.com

Swaptree
www.swaptree.com

Trade Your Stuff Online
www.tradeyourstuffonline.com

"Find Your Song" Power Songs

"Be Happy," Mary J. Bilge
"Brass in Pocket," The Pretenders
"Circle of Life," The Lion King
"Don't Stop," Fleetwood Mac
"Don't Stop Till You Get Enough," Michael Jackson
"Footloose," Kenny Loggins
"Groove Is in the Heart," Deee-Lite

"I Believe in a Thing Called Love," The Darkness
"I Will Survive," Gloria Gaynor
"I'm the Greatest Star," Barbra Streisand
"Life Is a Highway," Tom Cochrane
"Suddenly I See," K.T. Tunstall
"Sorry," Madonna
"These Boots Are Made for Walkin','" Nancy Sinatra
"This One's for the Girls," Martina McBride
"The Bitch Is Back," Elton John
"You Don't Own Me," Lesley Gore

AND FOR THE THINGS YOU DECIDE TO KEEP AND STORE:

Organization

California Closets
www.californiaclosets.com
1 (800) 274-6754

Closet Organizers USA
www.closetorganizersusa.com
1 (866) 418-1328

The Container Store
www.containerstore.com
1 (888) CONTAIN

Storage

Extra Space Storage
www.extraspace.com
1 (888) 586-9658

Public Storage
www.publicstorage.com
1 (877) 788-2028

If those aren't in your area, try Moving.com's self-storage search page:

www.moving.com

OTHER RESOURCES

Web Sites

www.partingwithpossessions.com

www.earth911.org

www.gotjunk.com

www.recycle.com

Magazines

Martha Stewart Living

Body + Soul

O: The Oprah Magazine

Organize

Real Simple

And, of course, the best resource for "throw-out" support is www.throwoutfiftythings.com. You can post your list of throw-outs and tell us how eliminating the physical and emotional debris has cleared your mind and restored your soul. You can also connect with a growing community of people who are letting go of the past, stepping into the future, and celebrating each other every inch of the way. And why not sing a few bars of your "power song"? Now, that would make a great video! "The Throw Out Fifty Things: Big Letting-Go Workbook" will be available online. Use it to keep track of your progress and remind yourself of how incredibly far you've come.

Index

A
affirmations
    for appreciating yourself, 123
    finding your song and
        singing it, 241–47
Amazon Kindle, 94
"angels," 198–205
    steps for finding angels in
        your life, 206–7
Astaire, Fred, 139–40
attic, 58–68
    "Attic Questionnaire," 66
    cleaning out a loved one's,
        63–65
    garage or tag sale, 59, 60
    memories in, 60, 61–62, 63,
        66
    saving items for your
        children, 59
    steps for clearing clutter, 67
    storage, resources, 159–60
    throw-out scorecard, 68

B
bathroom, 17–27
    expired drugs, disposing of,
        18
    hair and bath products, 25
    makeup, 21–24

medicine cabinet/
        prescription drugs,
        17–20, 26
    mental makeup throwaways,
        24
    mental medication
        throwaways, 20
    recycling makeup containers,
        22
    shower caddy, 25
    steps for clearing clutter,
        26–27
    throw-out scorecard, 27
batteries, 32
Beautiful Mind, A (film), xx–xxi
Becket, 127–28
Becket, Thomas, 128, 192
bedroom, 3–16
    closets, 7–12
    clothes, 4–5
    jewelry, xviii, 5–7, 15, 255
    Rules of Disengagement, 3
    steps for clearing clutter,
        14–15
    throw-out scorecard, 16
being unforgettable,
        232–40
    anticipate they'll love you,
        240

being unforgettable (*cont.*)
   charisma, acquiring, 237, 238
   communicating who you are, 233–35
   conviction, 238
   courage, 238
   let go of negative thoughts or fears, 239
   motivate and inspire, 239
   passion, 238
   shifting attention to the audience, 236–37, 239
   speak into the "listening" of your audience, 239–40
   steps for presenting yourself powerfully and being unforgettable, 238–39
Bernstein, Laurel, 200–201
bicycles, 70, 254
Bicycles for the World, 70
Big Letting-Go, xxi, 116
Bing, Sir Rudolf, 185–86
Blanke, Warren, 233–37
Blecher, Jane, 63–65, 67
Blodgett, Dan, 199, 201, 206
books, 40–43, 44–45, 93–94
   donating, resources, 45, 254
Books for Soldiers, 45
Brand, Stewart, 86
Brennan, Barbara, 5
Bridge of San Luis Rey, The (Wilder), 71
Brill, Eddie, 104–5
Bryan, William Jennings, 235

building materials, 254
Busby, Bob, 230

C
California Closets, 14, 259
Camp Farwell, Newbury, Vermont, 233
candles, 51–52
Carr, Sally, 74–79
Cartridge World, 91–92
cell phones, 254
Chairs, The (Ionesco), xxiv
Cher, 240
clarifying your brand, 85–96, 164–65
ClientWise, 228
Closet Organizers USA, 259
closets
   bedroom, 7–12
   organizing, resources, 259
   professional organizer for, 14
   story of Michael and the unopened envelope, 12–14
   total purge, 11–12
clothes, 4–5
   consignment shops, 115
   giving away, 6–7, 255
   single socks, xviii, 4
   swap party, 10
clothes hangers, metal, 112–13
color-coding throw-outs, 59
computer recycling, 104, 256
Comstock, Beth, 45, 92–95
Container Store, 14, 30, 81, 259
Curie, Marie, 139

D

Death of a Salesman (Miller),
161

declaration to the world, 248

defining moments, 223–31
author's Christmas ritual,
228
author's swim meet, 228–30
bride's choice, 224–27
list of, 231
Ray Sclafani's loss, 227–28
steps for celebrating your
courage, 231

digitizing documents, 100, 103,
257

dining room, 50–57
dishes and silverware, 53,
55–56
importance of family dining
together, 54
linens, 53
recycling old candles, 52
steps for clearing clutter,
55–56
throw-out scorecard, 56–57

Direct Mail Marketing
Association, 257

dishes and silverware, 53, 55–56

Disney, Walt, 214

donations, 53, 60, 61
bicycles, 70, 254
books, 94, 254
building materials, 254
cell phones, 254
clothes, 255
computers, 104, 256

electronics, 256
environmentally sensitive
materials, 256
food items, 256
jewelry, 255
organizations, general, for,
253–54
printer cartridges/toner,
91–92, 257
shoes, 8, 255
various goods, 257

Dumpster, 73–74

Durante, Jimmy, 137

E

Einstein, Albert, 120–21, 125,
178

Eldar, Lue Ann, 185–87

electronics, 256

Evangelista, David, 23

F

fears, xix
of failure, 138
throwing out fear that the
future won't be better, 110

feeling inadequate, irrelevant,
or not good enough,
119–26
affirmation, need for, 122
Albert Einstein and, 120–21
comparisons trap, 122–24
Olivia, example, 121–22
steps for letting go of
needless negative
comparisons and dump

feeling inadequate (*cont.*)
  feelings of inadequacy,
    125
  throw-out scorecard, 126
finding your song and singing
    it, 241–47
  author, "I'm the Greatest
    Star," 245–46
  cancer patient, overture from
    The Lion King, 244
  example of client, "My
    Sharona," 242–44
  job seeker, "The Bitch Is
    Back," 244–45
  power songs (list), 258–59
  steps for finding your song
    and singing it, 247

G
garage, 69–82
  bicycles, donating, 70, 254
  building materials, 254
  hazardous waste, 72–73, 256
  safely disposing of old paint,
    72
  steps for clearing clutter,
    80–81
  throw-out scorecard, 82
garage or tag sale, 48, 74–79, 81
  attic contents, 59, 67
  dishes, 52
  Mental Throwaways, 118
  Sally Carr's "Good Stuff" Tag
    Sale, 76–79
Gilliland, Martha, 102–4
Google, 94

green tips
  battery disposal, 32
  computer recycling, 104, 256
  expired prescription drugs, 18
  freon-containing appliances,
    61
  grocery bags, 30–31
  old ink and toner, 91–92, 257
  recycle your sneakers, 8, 255
  recycling makeup containers,
    22
  recycling old candles, 52
  recycling old televisions, 44,
    256
  safely disposing of old paint, 72
  throwing out hazardous
    waste, 72–73, 256
Gupta, Sanjay, 54

H
hairstyle, letting go of old, 23
hazardous waste, 72–73
Hoffman, David, 107–9, 224
hoshmahoken, 9, 116
Hough, Phil, 62
How Does It Make Me Feel? scale,
    112

I
In My Wildest Dreams (Blanke), 174
intentions, power of, 17–19
Ionesco, Eugene, xxiv

J
jewelry, 15
  costume, drawer of, 5–6

giving away, 6–7, 255
single earrings, xviii
Jobs, Steve, 85–87
website for commencement
speech, 87
John Barrett salon, 23
Jordan, Michael, 139
junk mail, 257

K
keeping what works, eliminating
what doesn't
eliminating nostalgia, 103–4
eliminating whatever weighs
you down or makes you
feel bad, 97–98
keeping objects associated
with memories, 102
keeping what gives us
pleasure, 97
letting go of old dreams,
103–4
purging yearly, 99–100
shredder, 100–101
steps for keeping what works
and eliminating what
doesn't, 105
throw-out scorecard, 106
keys, xviii–xix, 97
Kiehl's, 22
kitchen, 28–39
battery disposal, 32
donating food items, 256
food magazines, 28–29
junk drawer, xviii, 31–33
Marychris Melli's story,

34–36
pantry, 30
recipe for uncluttering,
28–29
steps for clearing clutter,
37–38
throw-out scorecard, 39
Klein, Parvin, 23–24

L
letting go of being right about
somebody/something
being wrong, 148–58
focusing on what is
important, 154–56
pressing the mental PAUSE
button, 151–52, 156
steps for letting go of needing
to be right, 157
throw-out scorecard, 158
letting go of needing to feel
secure, 190–96
adapting to change, 192
insecurity as good, 191
moving from our comfort
zones, 192–95
steps for letting go of the
need to be secure, 195
throw-out scorecard, 196
warm-up list for letting go,
193–94
letting go of the need to have
everyone like you, 159–68
avoiding controversy and, 160
clarifying your brand,
164–65

letting go of the need to have everyone like you (*cont.*)

list of qualities you like best about yourself, 164

list of things you're most proud of doing, 164

standing out instead of blending in, 161–62, 165

steps for letting go of needing everyone to like you, 167–68

throw-out scorecard, 168

letting go of thinking the worse (negative interpretations), 169–80

asking "What do I want to make happen?," 176, 178

evaluating major events of the past year, 179

list of what you want your life to be right now, 179

pressing the mental PAUSE button, 178

replacing with positive interpretation, 176

steps for clearing clutter of negative impressions, 179

throw-out scorecard, 180

letting go of thinking you have to do everything yourself, 197–207

appearance of "angels," 197, 198–205

steps for finding angels in your life, 206–7

throw-out scorecard, 207

letting go of type of person you think you are, or aren't, 127–36

list of "types," 134–35

recasting ourselves, 130–33, 136

steps for letting go of the type person you think you are, or aren't, 135–36

throw-out scorecard, 136

typecasting ourselves, 128–30

letting go of waiting for the right moment, 181–89

courage to move ahead, 184–85, 188

now is the right moment, 183

steps for letting go of waiting for the right moment, 188

throw-out scorecard, 189

lists to make. *See also* Mental Throw-outs list

for moving out of your comfort zone, 195

defining moments, 231

GOOD THINGS list, 144

insecurities, 195

losses, 188

"types," 134–35

wins, 188

what you want your life to be right now, 179

living room, 40–49

books, 40–43, 44–45

drawers in tables, 46

music (LPs, CDs), 43–44

photographs, 46–48
steps for clearing clutter,
48–49
television, 44
throw-out scorecard, 49
loss of possessions (rising from
the ashes), 107–10
single step for rising from
the ashes, 109
throw-out scorecard, 109

M
M*A*C, 22
magazine resources, 260
makeup, xviii
making a change, 21
recycling makeup containers,
22
reinventing yourself, 23–24
throwing out, 21–24
Matarasso, Alan, 172
Melli, Marychris, 34–36
memories
the attic and, 61–65, 66
celebrating, 33
divorce and, 113–16
family dining together and,
54
keeping objects associated
with, 11, 32, 53, 60,
61–62, 70–71, 72, 95, 102
keeping what gives us
pleasure, 97
storage, resources, 159–60
throwing out, 36
mental clutter, xix

bathroom mental
throwaways, 20, 24
Big Letting-Go, 116
fears, xix, 110
feeling inadequate,
irrelevant, or not good
enough, 119–26
form for throwing out, 250
letting go of being right
about somebody/
something being wrong,
148–58
letting go of needing to feel
secure, 190–96
letting go of the need to have
everyone like you, 159–68
letting go of negative
interpretations, 169–80
letting go of thinking the
worse, 169–80
letting go of thinking you
have to do everything
yourself, 197–207
letting go of type of person
you think you are, or
aren't, 127–36
letting go of waiting for the
right moment, 181–89
Mental Throw-Outs list,
134–35
physical clutter and, 112–18
regrets and mistakes of the
past, xix, 113–16, 137–47
resentments, xix
Rules of Disengagement for,
116–17

mental clutter (*cont.*)
voices in your head, xix–xx
mental makeup throwaways, 24
mental medication throwaways, 20
Mental Throw-Outs list
being right, 150–52, 156
comparisons trap, 123
having to do everything
yourself, 202
insecurities, 195
list of losses, 188
perfectionism, 146
phrase "as good as," 122
regrets and mistakes of the
past, 144, 146
"types" you are or are not,
134–35
waiting, 187
Michelangelo, 213–14, 241
Michelangelo Method, xv
Miller, Arthur, 161
Miller, Patricia, 51
Molko, David, 171
Murgolo, Karen, 170, 172

N
Nike's Reuse-A-Shoe, 8

O
office
books, 93–94
clarifying your brand, 85–96
clutter blurs clarity, 92
computer recycling, 104, 256
electronics, donating, 256
going paperless, 94–95

how long to keep what, 88–89
keeping objects associated
with memories, 95
old ink and toner, 91–92, 257
steps for clearing clutter,
95–96
throw-out scorecard, 96
official records, documents,
tax returns, and bank
statements, 88–89
digitizing, 100, 103, 257
shredder for, 100–101
Oprah Winfrey Show, The,
174–78

P
Perkins, Pat, 101–2
Perkins, Rod, 101–2
photographs, 46–48
scanning, 46
videotapes or DVDs of, 47
physical clutter
attic, 58–68
bathroom, 17–27
bedroom, 3–16
dining room, 50–57
garage, 69–82
kitchen, 28–39
list for, 249–50
living room, 40–49
mental clutter and, 112–18
office, 85–96
official records, documents,
tax returns, and bank
statements, 88–89, 100–
101, 103

Pine, Richard, 73, 202–3
power songs (list), 258–59
Preiss, Scott, 98–100
professional life
    clarifying your brand, 85–96
    keeping what works,
        eliminating what doesn't,
        97–110
    letting go of old dreams,
        103–4
    official records, documents,
        tax returns, and bank
        statements, 88–89,
        100–101, 103
    purging yearly, 99–100
    shredder, 100–101
    work-life balance issue,
        98–100

R
Radio Shack, 32
Rechargeable Battery Recycling
    Corporation, 32
recipes
    online sites, 29
    saving, 28–29
regrets and mistakes of the past,
    xix, 137–47
    divorce and, 113–16
    GOOD THINGS list, 144
    Jack, serious error in
        judgment, 140–44
    perfectionism and, 140, 146
    steps for letting go of your
        regrets and mistakes, 146
    throw-out scorecard, 147

reinventing yourself, 25–26
    clothes, 11–12
    hairstyle, 23–24
    makeup, 23
relationships
    Big Letting-Go, xxi
    divorce and regrets and
        mistakes of the past,
        113–16
Robb, Kathy, 98
routine purging, xxii, 5
Rules of Disengagement, xvii,
    xxiii
    Barbara Brennan's throw-out
        technique, 5
    bedroom, 3
    don't throw out other
        people's stuff, 29
    for mental clutter, 116–17

S
Sally Carr's "Good Stuff" Tag
    Sale, 76–79
Sclafani, Ray, 227–28
selling your things online, 258
shoes, 15
    donating, resources, 255
    recycle your sneakers, 8,
        255
shredder, 100–101
SiftSort, 88–89
Sony, 44
special finds, 250–51
Staples, 104
storage, resources, 259–60
Suzuki, Shin'ichi, 61–62

swapping your things
  online resources, 10
  swap party, 10
Sweet Briar College, 41–42

T
throw out fifty things, xxiv–xxvi
  color-coding throw-outs, 59
  DONATIONS bag, xxvii
  download workbook, xxv
  form for keeping track,
    250–51
  getting past memories, 63–65
  How Does It Make Me Feel? scale,
    112
  magazines and catalogs as one
    thing, xviii
  making it to fifty celebration,
    208–9
  materials needed to start,
    xxvi–xxvii, 63
  mental clutter and scoring, 118
  posting your list online,
    xxv–xxvi, 110, 208
  rag bag optional, xxvii
  Rules of Disengagement, 3
  SELL bag, xxvii
  time limit, xxvi

  TRASH bag, xxvii
  website, xxv
Throw Out Fifty Things Workbook, xxv,
    117, 260
trading your things, 258

V
vision for the future, 213–22
  boldness, 220
  career change, 218–20
  power of vision, 216
  set a date, 222
  steps to creating a vision,
    221–22
  vision exercises, 217–18
  what's your castle?, 214–15,
    219, 220–21, 222

W
warm-up list for moving out of
    your comfort zone, 195
Whole Earth Catalog, The (Brand), 86
Wilder, Thornton, 71
Winfrey, Oprah, 174–78

X
X-1, 94

About the Author

❖

Gail Blanke is a world-class motivator and is president and chief executive of Lifedesigns, a company whose vision is to empower men and women to live truly exceptional lives. She has been "The Motivator" columnist in *Real Simple* magazine; is a contributor to *Body + Soul*, a Martha Stewart publication; and appears regularly on *CBS 2 Sunday Morning*. Gail has written three other books, including *Between Trapezes* and *In My Wildest Dreams*, a *New York Times* bestseller. Gail and her husband, Jim Cusick, have two daughters, Kate and Abigail, and live in New York City.

You're invited to visit Gail at:
www.throwoutfiftythings.com.